THE
Entrepreneurial
BRAIN

HOW TO RIDE THE WAVES OF ENTREPRENEURSHIP AND LIVE TO TELL ABOUT IT

—

JEFF HAYS

HarperCollins
LEADERSHIP

AN IMPRINT OF HarperCollins

Published by HarperCollins Leadership, an imprint of HarperCollins Focus LLC.

Any internet addresses, phone numbers, or company or product information printed in this book are offered as a resource and are not intended in any way to be or to imply an endorsement by HarperCollins Leadership, nor does HarperCollins Leadership vouch for the existence, content, or services of these sites, phone numbers, companies, or products beyond the life of this book.

ISBN 978-1-4002-4322-8 (eBook)
ISBN 978-1-4002-4319-8 (TP)

Library of Congress Control Number: 2023936640

Printed in the United States of America
23 24 25 26 27 LBC 5 4 3 2 1

CONTENTS

INTRODUCTION

If you're going to invest your time in reading this book, you should know that I like sayings that get to the essence of important ideas. I keep a list of them in a notebook—and at the start of each chapter, I'm going to share one with you that seems relevant to the subject. A few are original, most are borrowed; I attribute them when I can. Here's your first . . . "A man with his health has a thousand dreams. A man without his health has only one."

n February 2005, I spoke about entrepreneurship to MBA students at the University of Utah's David Eccles School of Business. One of the students asked me if entrepreneurship could be taught.

"Yes," I said, "as long as you're teaching it to an entrepreneur."

What did I mean? That entrepreneurs aren't like everyone else. The way we process information makes us think and act differently. We have tremendous energy, drive, creativity, and confidence. Fueled by optimism, we see opportunities everywhere we look and we're quick to take advantage of them. This is both a gift and a burden in life, an advantage and a disadvantage, and it means that the stakes we play for are high.

It also means that learning how to make the most of your strengths while managing your weaknesses can be more than a matter of financial success and failure; your health and wellness are on the line too. I know, because I've learned the hard way. That, more than anything else, is why I'm writing this book.

I once had a conversation with Dr. Edward M. "Ned" Hallowell, a psychiatrist renowned for his expertise in the field of ADHD (attention deficit hyperactivity disorder), who made the stakes very clear. "It's sort of like you have a Ferrari engine for a brain," he said. "You've got a really powerful race car for a brain. You're very lucky. You have this amazingly powerful engine up there. But you have bicycle brakes. . . .

"A Ferrari with no brakes is pretty dangerous, but a Ferrari with brakes wins races."

I've known I was different my entire life, but I didn't get a measurement of how different until I took the Kolbe Index Personality Assessment some years ago. The test has four categories. One is called Quick Start, which measures how quickly you assess and tolerate risk and move forward. Entrepreneurs always score very high in this category, often getting a seven, eight, or nine. Those who get tens are unicorns. I got a ten. This isn't something to brag about. It's simply a measure of extreme behavior.

On the Follow Through section I got a two. That means that I'm really good at starting projects but not very good at finishing them. It's a common trait among entrepreneurs.

And that's not all that sets us apart.

THE WAYS WE'RE DIFFERENT

Entrepreneurs will get really excited about something, but then we quickly lose interest and move on to the next thing. We're easily distracted. Some of us will read more than a handful of books at the same time, bouncing from one to another just as we jump from one business idea to the next. Others don't read at all. One thing I've noticed about entrepreneurs is that a staggering number of us are dyslexic.

Our entrepreneurial brains run on momentum. We are notorious for building companies, then destroying them from the inside. We do this because our creativity and need for momentum never stop—or we simply grow bored. We'll often encourage our teams to abandon a half-finished project and move on to the next one. If we're not careful, we may end up building foundations of companies all over the place, and then lose out when other people swoop in and capitalize on our ideas.

Entrepreneurs also tend to talk a lot. Talking is our way of processing information. When we say things out loud, our ears take in the information and our brains reprocess it. We learn much easier this way. When I was younger, I would say, "How do I know what I feel until I hear what I say?" People would laugh, but I wasn't joking.

We have an amazing ability to see the big picture but are terrible at keeping track of details. We're often able to do complicated math problems in our heads, but we're unable to tell you how we did them. Fortunately, the ability to do math quickly in our heads is an advantage in the business world. A controller who worked for me for five years liked to create elaborate spreadsheets. If something was wrong with one of them, I could tell right away. I couldn't tell him where the error was, but I could say without a doubt that something wasn't right. This ability doesn't mean I'm smarter than anyone else. It just means that I have a faster processing speed.

That relates to something else entrepreneurs often have in common: struggles in school.

Our public school system was designed and funded in the early 1900s by the Carnegies and Rockefellers. Their objective was to prepare people for factory work. Our school system continues to reflect this. Teachers usually score very high on the Follow Through section of the Kolbe test but low on the Quick Start section. They are detail-oriented and expect the same from their students. Creativity is not taught or valued. Neither is big-picture thinking. What's valued is sitting still, paying attention, memorizing facts and figures, putting the right number in the right box, and being able to show your work.

To teachers, we look like we're broken, but that's not necessarily the case. Our brains are simply different. For a child with an entrepreneurial brain, the result can be devastating. I'm a high school dropout. At the time I felt there was something wrong with me, when in reality I just didn't fit into the school system.

Bill Gates dropped out of school before graduating. The famed venture capitalist Peter Thiel created a foundation that actually pays people not to go to college so they can get a real education.

Cameron Herold is the founder of the COO Alliance and the man responsible for the exponential growth of hundreds of companies, including 1-800-GOT-JUNK? He has a very high IQ but struggled in school too.

"There are different subsets of the community or society that are just wired differently," Herold told me. "We have this group of people that are very entrepreneurial, the outliers, the 3 to 4 percent that everyone looks at as being risk takers and crazy and out of the box and we can't sit still and we're all over the map and we're scattered, and to the teachers and the school system and the medical community they think we're a little bit nuts. They think there's something wrong with us, and they often try to medicate us. The reality is that there's nothing wrong with us at all. We're just not like them."

THE PLACES WE GO

Those who have entrepreneurial brains feel like the rules don't apply to them. When somebody tells us we can't do something—for example, we shouldn't start a company but should go to college and get a 9–5 job instead—we tend to ignore them.

Believing we're different encourages us to skip the traditional path to success, and very often we go on to accomplish extraordinary things. That's the positive side of this trait. Unfortunately, believing that the rules don't apply to you is also a good way to end up in jail. Our country's prisons are full of people with entrepreneurial brains. Entrepreneurs might succeed without school, but we can't succeed without a moral compass, values, and proper guidance.

We are Ferraris. And we'll crash if we don't develop our brakes.

What does that mean, exactly? For one thing, we can be as good at losing fortunes as we are at making them. In 1998, James Altucher, the hedge fund manager, entrepreneur, and venture capitalist, sold his first company, Reset Inc., for roughly $15 million. Three and a half years later, he had less than $150 in his bank account. That didn't stop him. He created StockPickr, a social network for financial news and analysis, and in 2007 he sold it for $10 million. Within just a few years of the sale, he was broke once again. With company after company, success or failure, he lived on a tightrope of high risk-tolerance and extreme self-confidence. Every time he fell off, he'd get on again. A *Forbes* article once called him the most interesting man in the world, which had mixed meanings. Fortunately, with time James learned to manage his own tendencies. I'll have more to share about how he came to that wisdom later.

As entrepreneurs, we see choices differently than others do. Ray Kroc is the entrepreneur credited with turning McDonald's into the global franchise it is today, and he's not always celebrated for it. In the film *The Founder*, Kroc is portrayed as a man who victimized the McDonald brothers. As their relationship is depicted in the movie, the McDonald brothers cared more about quality than growth. Kroc saw that by dropping the quality just a little and selling milkshakes made from powder, they could rapidly expand the business. Kroc is seen as the villain of the story. But that's not how I saw him, because I could picture myself in his shoes.

Incidentally, I was embarrassed by my reaction; it was a bit like watching *The Sopranos* and realizing that you really like Tony Soprano. But how would I respond if I saw an opportunity to create a multibillion-dollar company and the people I had partnered with were committed to staying small? Would I let that opportunity pass by? Not a chance. I don't see anyone as the bad guy in the McDonald's story.

Of course, if you're driving without brakes, there's more than money on the line. In 2015, Elizabeth Holmes, the CEO of the blood-testing start-up Theranos, was acclaimed as the youngest, wealthiest female billionaire in America. In 2018 she found herself facing criminal charges for defrauding investors in a case that ended in a settlement in which she paid a $500,000 fine, returned millions of shares to the company, and agreed to yield control of the company. Theranos is now defunct. Holmes had many of the traits that typify successful entrepreneurs: She dropped out of Stanford, had a vision, refused to let people dissuade her, and kept moving forward. She didn't set out to commit fraud. Unfortunately, the vision she had wasn't technically possible at the time. Her entrepreneurial brain refused to let that stop her, assuring her that she could solve the problem. She intended to do something amazing; instead she crashed, and her company did too.

For an entrepreneurial brain without brakes, even the heights of success can bring tragedy. Tony Hsieh became a legend as the leader of Zappos, the online shoe and clothing retailer he sold to Amazon for more than a billion dollars.

He was celebrated for putting his inspirational, worker- and customer-centered values at the core of the company's success. He wrote a bestselling book on company culture titled *Delivering Happiness,* and the truth is that he was a master of the art—for everyone but himself. The traits that drove his business success also drove him to self-destructive behavior: alcohol, drugs, and extreme diets. After leaving Zappos, Hsieh died in 2020 at the age of forty-six. He perished in a house fire following six months of what the *Wall Street Journal* described as a "downward spiral."

Those of us with entrepreneurial brains are capable of great things. I wouldn't give mine up if I could. But our capabilities alone don't guarantee success, nor do they doom us to failure. If you've got an entrepreneurial brain, you have a gift. Making the most of it requires help.

MEET MY MENTOR
DAVID NEMELKA

Another thing you should know if we're going to hang out together: Throughout the course of this book, I want you to get to know my greatest mentor, David Nemelka. In each chapter you'll find a story that captures aspects of his wisdom. Some will be related to the chapter content, others won't, but together they'll paint a picture, and I think you'll be surprised by what I tell you about him when we get to the end. Anyway, here's how we met:

My wife at the time and I had six kids, one of whom was terminally ill with cancer. We thought it was his last year of life. We were living in Dallas and decided to take the winter off from work and move to Park City, Utah, for the ski season. We rented a house, got ski passes, put the kids in school there, and spent the winter as a family.

The neighbor across the street, John Hewlett, walked over to introduce himself. He's become a lifelong friend, and as he got to know everything I was handling, John said, "I need to introduce you to David Nemelka, the best father I've ever known."

I called and asked for an appointment.

"My time is all booked up; I've literally got no extra hours," David told me. "But if you'll get here at ten thirty tonight, I'll give you some of my sleep time."

David lived ninety minutes away in Mapleton, Utah, in a spectacular twenty-thousand-square-foot house at the base of a mountain. When I got there, he was still on the phone working, so, I waited until eleven o'clock—and then he gave me two hours.

He spent the first hour getting to know me. "Tell me about your family," he began. As we talked, I realized he was using an old-school system of building rapport called FORM: family, occupation, recreation, marriage.

Then he began telling me stories about raising kids. Two of his sons went to the Wharton School (of the University of Pennsylvania), a daughter was studying law at Brigham Young University, another son also became a lawyer, and another child graduated from the University of Chicago with an MBA. David had been a social worker, a state legislator, and had literally helped rescue kids on drugs by bringing them into his home. He was a *spectacular* father.

From that night forward, I visited David every two weeks for six months. He evolved into my mentor and a key investor in most of my businesses—and it all began when he gave me two hours of his sleep time.

GETTING STARTED

By the time I was ten, I was selling seeds from an ad I found in the back of *Boys' Life* magazine (later renamed *Scout Life*)—work that quickly taught me the difference between gross and net. When I was twelve, I started a paper route. At eighteen, after a few years on the road with a rock 'n' roll band, I began selling encyclopedias door-to-door. Next I sold siding the same way. At twenty-five, I started my own direct sales company, selling water softeners, and at twenty-eight, I founded a brokerage firm. When I was thirty-six, I started my own film company—and I've been bringing an entrepreneurial mindset to documentary filmmaking ever since. I have made and lost millions and learned a good deal about life with an entrepreneurial brain along the way. I've picked up a lot of lessons also, and I'm excited to share them.

In Part One, I'm going to give you some insight into the mindset entrepreneurs need to develop in order to survive. And when I say *survive*, I mean it: your money, your relationships, your sanity, and even your life are at stake if you don't come to understand why you are the way you are, and how to manage it.

Part Two is about tactics and strategies—specific tools you can use in business to enjoy even more success than you've imagined while avoiding some of the pitfalls along the way. I've learned the pitfalls the hard way, letting my entrepreneurial brain drive me off a cliff over and over again. Failure has been one of my greatest teachers, showing me how to work with my brain and how to work with others. My goal is to help you experience all the ups, and more, while protecting yourself against some of the downs.

Our country was settled by entrepreneurs. To get on a boat, sail across the ocean, and start an entirely new life in an uncharted territory required a high tolerance for risk. Many of the Founding Fathers of the United States frequently displayed behavior commonly exhibited by those with entrepreneurial brains. They had high risk tolerance and delusions of grandeur and were incredibly optimistic—and thank God for that because people who lacked this combination of traits would never have had the audacity to stand up to the British and build a new country from scratch. These traits were passed down to the first generation of Americans, who weren't content to stay on the East Coast and work as laborers for someone else. In search of opportunities, they migrated west and became blacksmiths, shopkeepers, and cattle ranchers. Self-made businesspeople. Entrepreneurs.

The world needs people with all kinds of brains. Because I'm all about the big picture, I need detail-oriented people around me to succeed. Because I'm thinking-oriented, I need action-oriented people by my side. But this isn't a book for the detail- and action-oriented except in how it may help them better understand people with entrepreneurial brains like mine.

If you've got an entrepreneurial brain, too, you are not broken. Far from it. You're unique, creative, gifted. You are exactly who you're supposed to be, and with the right kind of help you can succeed in all meanings of the word. I believe there's never been a better time to be an entrepreneur, because one of the key aspects of our personalities, our creativity, has never been more valued. Offering insights based on what I've learned through experience is my way of serving as a mentor for you, just as David Nemelka and others you'll meet along the way were for me.

Let's get started.

THE
Entrepreneurial
BRAIN

PART ONE

MINDSET

1

FAILURE, YOUR INEVITABLE COMPANION

If you're not earning, you better be learning.

(FROM JEFF'S NOTEBOOK)

Here's something you need to know about business and, I'm afraid, about life too: you're going to fail. It's inescapable. So, the question is not simply how to avoid failure, but how to think of it, and how to keep it from crippling you. I'm an admirer of an approach to therapeutic learning called neuro-linguistic programming. Though it has its critics, I find value in its core concepts, including this one: the language you use frames your thinking, beliefs, and feelings. One of NLP's twenty-seven presuppositions is that there are no failures, only outcomes. With experience I've come to recognize that, while failure can be bruising and bitter, it's not necessarily bad. That's especially so if you prepare your mind and your spirit for the possibility of failure and learn to mitigate its consequences while absorbing the lessons it teaches. That's what this chapter is about.

In October 1996, I went on a three-day bike ride on the White Rim Trail in Utah's Canyonlands National Park. Riding this trail had become a rite of passage for my kids. Once they turned twelve, they were old enough to join me on this hundred-mile ride, which requires you to camp each night and use support vehicles to carry your food, water, and gear.

This area is famous for its beautiful canyons, arches, and slick rock, but I was having a hard time enjoying it because I was riding with a broken heart. On September 1, my wife had told me she wanted a divorce. Just seventeen days later, under a new Utah law that made divorce final upon filing in cases with no financial or property disputes, I became a single father.

About halfway through the Canyonlands ride, I was by myself on a flat section of slick rock with amazing views in every direction when I was struck by the most brilliant business idea I'd ever had. I stopped, got off my mountain bike, and started jumping up and down and yelling as loud as I could. That moment of inspiration would become a company named Talk2Technologies—leveraging the then-novel concept of viral marketing to create the world's first voice portal to the internet. I thought I'd taken a billion-dollar bike ride.

The next six months were the hardest of my life. My son Charlie died in January 1997. Three months later, my dad died, too, and I was hit with a $2 million tax lien. I lost my house and cars and was completely broke. I was wiped out both financially and emotionally. But I had my billion-dollar business idea. Besides my children, it was the only thing that kept me going.

I pitched my mentor, David Nemelka, and he agreed to invest $100,000. Following his suggestion, I brought in three other partners, and each of us split the remaining stock of a company named Talk2Technologies four ways. We patented the idea of "virus marketing," and we went on to build the first voice portal to the internet, using voice recognition just as Siri and Alexa do today.

Fueled by the 1990s internet boom, we raised $75 million for the company. At one point, we ran a full-page ad in the *Wall Street Journal* that cost $100,000. The first line of copy read, "Dear John, Bernie, and Ed." "John" was John T. Chambers, CEO of Cisco Systems. "Bernie" was Bernie J. Ebbers, CEO of WorldCom. (He later served thirteen years of a twenty-five-year sentence for defrauding investors.) And "Ed" was Edward J. Zander, president and COO of Sun Microsystems. The rest of the ad basically said, "Hey, we're doing something really cool and you guys should be part of it. Call us."

Everyone called. Larry Ellison, the cofounder of Oracle Corporation, invested; and Hewlett-Packard and Sun Microsystems got in a bidding war to see which would invest in the company. We ended up going with HP, which gave us $10 million in computers. Of the $75 million we raised, $10 million went to building a state-of-the-art network operations center in Salt Lake City.

We were off and running—or so we thought. I'll finish the story later. First, let me share a story about David and then two of the key lessons I've learned about handling failure.

DAVID'S WISDOM
IT'S NOT WHETHER THEY'RE LOVED . . .

This is one of my David Nemelka stories. It's not related to the chapter content. But it's beautiful.

Time after time, when I was having a problem with one of my kids, I would drive to Mapleton, sit with David, and watch him think it through. David always used farm and nature metaphors to explain his thinking.

"Jeff, if you have a tree that gets bent by the wind," he said, "you need to tie it to a stake for a while as it gains strength. Once it's strong, you don't need the tie. But if it is going to bend or break again, it tends to do so in the same spot."

When my stepson Dane was in junior high school, I'd get calls from his teacher telling me that he'd fallen asleep during class. David's advice: Go to his class, pull up a chair, and sit next to him. If he falls asleep, lift his head.

Sure enough, Dane had to test it. When the teacher called again, I drove to the junior high, pulled up a chair, and sat with my arm around him to make sure he stayed awake. It only took a couple of times before he got the message.

It wasn't actually about keeping him awake during class. The real message was that I loved him enough to take the time to sit beside him in class, humiliating as that was for him.

"It's not whether you love the kids," David said. "It's whether they feel loved."

HEDGE YOUR BETS

By definition, entrepreneurs are optimists, and most behave as if failure isn't an option. That couldn't be more wrong. Failure is always an option. You obviously don't set out to fail, and you shouldn't be thinking about failing while you're working on an idea, but you do need to be honest with yourself about the level of risk you're taking on and be prepared in case your idea flops. It's essential that we understand the pitfalls we're inevitably going to face.

Here's why I say this: No one marries planning to divorce, but wealthy singles now routinely get prenups, and for good reason. Half of marriages end in divorce. As an entrepreneur, your chances are worse. Nine out of ten new businesses fail within the first five years. That's fact. Sooner or later, you're going to fail, and you're likely to fail often.

If you're always willing to push all your chips onto the table, eventually you're going to lose them—every last one. Even if you're right three times in a row, a failure the fourth time will wipe you out. I was a multimillionaire by the age of twenty-nine and broke by the time I was thirty-one.

I've had more than a few years where I've made millions followed by years where I've lost everything.

Entrepreneurs are notorious for this. After making $100 million from PayPal, Elon Musk went all in on two moon shots—SpaceX and Tesla. At one point, he was so broke he was sleeping on a friend's couch. Fortunately for him, Tesla eventually turned the corner. As a result, he's now the poster child for entrepreneurs. If Tesla hadn't turned itself around—and it's still not completely out of the woods yet—Musk would be looked on as one of the greatest fools in business history. His is a terribly dangerous model, and most people who follow it will go right off the cliff.

There are ways to play this game without taking a $100 million windfall, risking it all, and losing so much of it you end up on a friend's couch. It all begins with your approach.

WHEN YOU LOSE, LEARN

If you embrace the philosophy that there are no failures, only outcomes, putting it into action begins with being purposeful. Think of everything you do in the market-place as a test; if it fails, you advance your understanding. Structure your initiatives so there are only two outcomes: you either succeed or you learn something. Google ranks among the highly successful companies that have made an art of this; it actually rewards its teams for failing fast, by proving that an idea doesn't work at low cost and putting it behind them. That makes your next test more likely to succeed. You've kept most of your chips off the table. You've bought knowledge, and that makes you more valuable than you were before.

I've learned to apply this methodology to my smallest ideas as well as my biggest. Once I was planning to offer a free webinar to one of my email lists as a tool for selling a product that cost $2,000. Before I did, I called my business coach at the time, Roger Hamilton, the creator of the Wealth Dynamics experience.

He said, "If you roll out a webinar and it fails, you won't have learned anything. The only way to do it is as a test launch. Don't roll it out to your whole list. Roll it out to part of the list. Get the numbers and see if it works. If it doesn't work, you haven't lost because you've learned."

If the webinar had failed, there could have been a dozen reasons for it. It would have taken multiple iterations to get it right. If I hadn't taken Roger's advice and left myself some runway for further testing, I wouldn't have been able to fix it.

The webinar ended up being a successful six-figure promotion because we were right. It did work. But if I had launched it to my whole list, it could have easily led to failure. Better to run lots of small tests and to fail faster, to embrace small failures and avoid the catastrophic ones.

THE SLEEPLESS NIGHTS

I wish I could tell you that I've always hedged my bets and structured everything I've done as a test, that I've never pushed all my chips to the center of the table. But I can't tell you that.

You'll remember Talk2Technologies, my billion-dollar bike-ride idea. We raised our $75 million from venture capitalists and leading tech companies, and we spent our money building our voice portal to the internet. These were the days of waterfall development; you built and built behind closed doors, intent on guarding your secrets from competitors, and when at last it was ready, out and over the waterfall it went.

Our idea was way ahead of its time, and the technology wasn't mature. You'd tell it, "Call my lawyer," and it would say, "Calling your mother-in-law." We ended up selling Talk2Technologies for $10 million. It was a spectacular torching of capital, and our investors paid the price.

Was that enough to teach me the lesson? Unfortunately, no. By 2005, I had created and immersed myself in another company that was ahead of its time: Podfitness, a service that made customized workouts that could be downloaded from an iPod. I raised $25 million for the company and spent much of it building a computer system that could assemble the audio files so that each customer could get a unique audio workout every day.

Our enthusiasm for our idea knew no bounds. As soon as we had the first version of Podfitness set for release, I took out a full-page ad nationwide in the *Wall Street Journal* and had a six-foot version of it delivered to Steve Jobs's office. "Dear Steve Jobs," the title said. "Thanks for the iPod." I signed it and added this PS: "Wait till you hear what we did with it! Call me . . ." after which I added my cell phone number. We added a picture of our product, our website, and a few words about our service and its pricing.

The next day we heard from about thirty fitness industry leaders who wanted to talk about working with us. We
heard from Apple's legal department too—with a cease-and-
desist letter claiming the rights to "pod" and insisting that
we change our name.

My response was complete indignation. Apple hadn't
filed for a trademark on "pod" and I was certain we had
every right to use it.

My ad cost $125,000 to run nationwide. My indignation
cost $1 million.

Apple sued, we fought back—and proceeded to get our
butt kicked in court for a year. In the process, Apple taught
me what it's like to fight with a giant, and after a million
dollars spent learning that lesson, I was ready to settle the
lawsuit. But Apple wanted to make us an example for anyone
else who was tempted to use the word "pod."

I fired my San Francisco law firm in favor of two Salt
Lake City lawyers who were meaner than junkyard dogs.
They proceeded to pepper Apple with motions. They prepared me so well that when Apple's lawyers came to town
to depose me, it was a piece of cake. During the deposition,
a bitter snowstorm swept in, and when we were done I
gave them a ride to their hotel. Maybe it was the motions,
maybe it was my performance, maybe it was the ride—I
don't know—but a couple of months later they let us out of
the suit. Two years after we filed suit, we gave up the name
"pod" in favor of "next," and became Nextfitness.

And in the end, none of that mattered.

Only after we started selling the product did we discover
that the thing that was most important to me—delivering

a customized workout to each customer—was the thing customers cared about the least. They didn't care if it was customized or not. Podfitness, Nextfitness, neither mattered to them. They just wanted a great workout. We were on the road to failure by any name.

There were times when I'd lie in bed on a Thursday night literally sweating and wondering, "How am I going to come up with the money to make payroll tomorrow?" We might owe our employees as much as $150,000 on a Friday, and we wouldn't raise the money until four o'clock that afternoon.

A low point came when I had to sell a beautiful Harley-Davidson motorcycle for a fraction of the original price I'd paid—$27,000—in order to make the final bit of payroll.

People used to ask me, "What does it take to be a successful entrepreneur?"

"Every drop of your blood," I would answer.

I was wrong. Achieving success only takes every drop of your blood if you let it, and you shouldn't. I had a girlfriend years ago who told me: "Jeff, you've had to fight for everything you've ever had in life. But not everything is a fight." She has since passed away, and I still love her for that insight. It was one of the most beneficial lessons I've ever been taught. Not everything is a fight. Certainly that can only mean that not everything is a fight to the death either.

2

EMBRACE PARADOX

You can't perform a noble act
without becoming more noble,
even if you do a noble act against your will.

(FROM JEFF'S NOTEBOOK)

n the second half of this book, I'm going to share a number
of business strategies, and half of them are paradoxical—
outlining two seemingly contradictory approaches that
both happen to be true. I've learned this is a good thing, not
a bad one. I'm far from the first person to stumble into that
insight. Niels Bohr was a Danish physicist and one of the
great thinkers of the twentieth century. "How wonderful
that we have met with a paradox," he once said. "Now we
have some hope of making progress."

My business partner, Patrick Gentempo, defines a paradox as a statement or proposition that seems contradictory
or absurd but expresses a higher truth. That's not to be

mistaken for a contradiction: a statement, value, or proposition that denies another and is logically incongruent.

A paradox is an open door to transcendence. A contradiction is a brick wall. Paradoxes help you grow; contradictions keep you small. Once you embrace paradox, you'll find yourself playing at a higher level.

All that's pretty abstract, the kind of stuff a theoretical physicist like Bohr would love, so let me bring it down to earth.

I was once a member of a mastermind group—a gathering of successful internet marketers who met four times a year. The group itself was the heart of a very successful marketing business that grew by leaps and bounds. At every gathering, the members of the group drew back the curtain on their own operations, describing what worked, what didn't, and what they learned from it. At about the time they were surging from $50 million to $100 million in sales, I found their advice no longer useful or relevant to me and my company and our $5 million in business. They had grown up and left me. The things a company needs to do to grow from $50 million to $100 million have very little relationship to what it needs to do to go from $5 million to $10 million, and almost nothing to do with how to go from zero to a million. It's not that the advice they gave us was wrong; it just wasn't the right advice for me at the time. After all, if you're traveling from New York to Los Angeles and you ask how far it is, then drive to St. Louis and ask again, you get a different answer. The person in St. Louis is not lying; you're just in a different place.

When you start a business, you need to do everything; if you don't, you will fail. If the business succeeds and you're still the one doing everything, you will fail. That's a paradox, but your responsibilities must shift as your business grows. (Imagine if Richard Branson had to build the rockets and fly the airplanes.)

Let's talk about some of the other paradoxical principles I've learned to respect.

NEVER QUIT . . . UNLESS YOU SHOULD

I was taught at an early age that quitting meant failure and that you should never give up. The Never Quit philosophy got me started. I worked for a rock band called Thunderhead for three years beginning when I was sixteen. They had an album out on ABC Records and were on the road all the time. When we had a show, it didn't matter if the electricity went out or the car broke down on the way there. No excuse for not playing was acceptable. We were putting on a show.

After my rock days ended, I cut off a foot of hair and went to work as a door-to-door salesman selling encyclopedias in Lubbock, Texas. We only got paid if we made a sale, so "Never Quit" became my motto. On weekdays our sales manager would drive us around town in a Chevy Suburban, drop us off somewhere at 5:00 p.m., and pick us up at 10:00 p.m. We usually worked two shifts on Saturday and Sunday. It didn't matter if it was pouring rain, 105 degrees outside, or the Fourth of July. In fact, the Fourth was our biggest sales day of the year. The company paid us extra commission on sales, and we knew everybody would be home.

We had a code phrase for impossible situations—"Hey, man, we're on the whatever-it-takes program"—and we lived by it. One day our manager drove us to Bovina, Texas, and his Suburban's transmission went out along the way. Reverse still worked, though. So, he dropped us off while driving around town backward. When he discovered that all the service stations in Bovina had closed at 5:00 p.m., he drove in reverse on the side of the highway all the way to Clovis, New Mexico, where it was an hour earlier because it was in the Mountain Time Zone. There he found a service station that was still open, got the transmission fixed, and picked us up right on time at 10:00 p.m.

"Whatever it takes" worked for us. I bought my first Cadillac with the money I earned selling those encyclopedias door-to-door.

The Never Quit philosophy has paid great dividends for others too. In 1977, Greg Bonann was working as a lifeguard at California's Will Rogers State Beach when he rescued two kids who'd gotten caught in a riptide. Their father was Stu Erwin, one of the most successful television executives in the country, and he was so grateful he told Greg, "If there's anything I can ever do for you, please let me know." Taking him up on the offer, Greg pitched him the idea of a television show about his life as a lifeguard, full of beautiful people and dramatic rescues. At the end of the pitch, Erwin looked at Greg and said, "I've got to tell you—that was the worst presentation of a show I've ever heard."

Unfazed, Greg pitched that show every chance he got for the next ten years, and he got one rejection after another. One of the people who turned him down was Grant Tinker, but ten years after Tinker's first rejection, Greg managed to get in front of him again. By then Tinker had been brought in to run NBC, and Greg had gotten a lot better at making his pitch. Tinker actually bought the show. Unfortunately for Greg, it was canceled after just one season.

On Father's Day that year, Greg's father stopped by his house. "All I want for Father's Day," he told his son, "is for you to go to Grant Tinker and ask him to sell you your show back."

"Dad, that's not how television works," said Greg, "After you sell a show, you don't get it back."

His dad was adamant, so, the next day, Greg got an appointment to meet with Tinker and this time he pitched him the idea of selling him back his show. Tinker walked out of the room, came back with some paperwork, and said, "Write me a check for ten bucks."

"Why?" Greg asked.

"Because I can't give it to you for free," said Tinker. He was right; to be legal, the transaction required a payment. Greg had to pay something.

Next, Greg took *Baywatch* outside the box. He hired a sales team and had them sell the show directly to local television stations on first run syndication. No one had done that before; syndication had always followed a network run that built an audience. Greg turned the model upside down. His team sold to markets across the United States and as many as they could abroad as well. Greg's philosophy was, "If a country is big enough to send a team to the Olympics, we'll sell to them." That's how *Baywatch* became the number one show in places like Afghanistan, Iran, and Iraq and eventually the most successful show in television history.

For ten solid years Greg was advised to quit. Fortunately, he never did.

So, does the Never Quit philosophy work? Absolutely— unless it doesn't. Remember, we're talking about paradoxes here.

I told you about Podfitness in Chapter 1. I lost $25 million on the company because I'd been trained to never give up. I spent $7 million to develop the product before putting it in front of customers, and $18 million more after a first test suggested it wasn't what customers wanted at the time. I was offering a customized personal workout, tailored to their needs, voiced by celebrities and generated by computer. The day for that would come, but in 2005 it was far in the future. Back then, people just wanted a good workout. For a half-million dollars, we could have built something smaller, less capable, and less robust and used it to get feedback from customers. There's no question what we'd have learned. As much as any experience I've had, Podfitness taught me that there comes a time when the best move *is* quitting. You might call that approach Hurry Up and Quit.

Never Quit? Yes. Hurry Up and Quit? That's a yes too.

TO MAKE MORE, GIVE MORE

The objective of any business is making money. That's what you're there to do, and if you can't do it, at some point you'll no longer be able to keep trying. But I've learned that the best way to get there isn't always a straight line. In fact, one of the best ways I've found to make money is to delight your customers by giving them content for free.

In 2013, I made a movie called *Bought* about the connection between vaccines, Big Pharma, and food. There was a lot of buzz surrounding the film, so we decided to release it ourselves on a video-on-demand platform called Yekra. We ran a marketing test to determine the right price to charge customers to stream the film online. The options were $1.95, $4.95, and $6.95. I figured $1.95 would test the best, but much to my surprise it performed the worst. People simply didn't believe they could watch a good movie for $1.95. The winner was $4.95.

We were confident *Bought* would be successful, because we had two thousand affiliates talk up the film to everyone on their email lists. No film on Yekra had ever been promoted by so many affiliates. We gave Yekra a six-week exclusive, and during those six weeks we made a grand total of $60,000—on a film that took $750,000 to make.

Earning back less than 10 percent of your cost is no one's idea of success.

So, we retooled. After Yekra closed down the following year, we created the website boughtmovie.com, reached out to our affiliates, and offered a free ten-day screening period. If you wanted to see the film, you didn't have to pay a dime. All we asked in return was for you to give us your email address. During that ten-day period, we had 250,000 people register to see *Bought*, and a good percentage of them liked it enough to buy the DVD. We ended up making $220,000 on DVD sales.

But that was just the start, because now we had an email list with 250,000 people on it. We went on to bring in $2 million in revenue. That same list continues to generate hundreds of thousands of dollars of revenue each year.

The more content we gave away, the more we made. Embracing this paradox, we started producing docuseries. Now, instead of allowing viewers to watch one of our films free for ten days, we produce a docuseries that's twenty hours long and we give away the first episode for free for twenty-four hours, then do the same for subsequent episodes. We began giving away ten times as much content but also making ten times as much money, while expending the same amount of effort we had making films.

This model is similar to the one used by Andy Weir, who wrote the science fiction novel *The Martian*. Having seen previous books he'd written get rejected by a bunch of literary agents, Weir decided to give away one chapter of *The Martian* at a time on his website. When that generated a lot of excitement among his fans, he sold a Kindle version of the book on Amazon for ninety-nine cents, and it sold 35,000 copies in three months. Weir ended up selling the print rights of his book to Crown Publishing for more than $100,000. After that, the book was on the *New York Times* Best Seller list and made into a movie starring Matt Damon.

There are very few wealthy documentary filmmakers, but I'm one of them. I credit the fact that I think and act differently than other documentary filmmakers, because I've been willing to embrace a paradox.

DAVID'S WISDOM
REPUBLICAN TURNS DEMOCRAT

Back in the seventies, David got angry about an injustice he saw and decided to do something about it. He set out to run for the Utah state legislature. He was a Republican, and he put his hat in the ring. What followed was a visit from the Republican powers that be. They told him it wasn't his turn, that the party had already selected someone else, and they asked David to stand down.

David was obstinate. "I'm not about taking turns," he said. "I'm running."

With the Republican infrastructure against him, he ran as a Democrat. And he beat the guy the Republicans wanted.

David thought he had won the battle, but once in the legislature, he got nothing done. The Republicans, who were in the majority, completely froze him out. He wasn't able to accomplish anything.

"Okay," he said, "now I know how it plays." At the end of his two-year term, David ran again—and this time he put Democrats up in other districts and helped them develop their campaigns. He won again—and so did most of the people he supported. It was the first—and last—time the Utah state legislature was controlled by Democrats. David got his agenda done—and won the legislature's Don Quixote Award for fighting the battles of the less fortunate as a result.

That's a Never Quit story, but it comes with a paradox: if you can't beat your fellow Republicans, be a
Democrat.

TO MULTIPLY, DIVIDE

In 2017, Patrick Gentempo and I launched a docuseries
called *Christ Revealed*. After we finished it, I moved on to
other projects. We'd built an email list of six hundred thousand evangelical Christians, and every time we launched the
series we added to the list, and the series made money. But
in 2019, we didn't have time to launch the series even once,
so it was a completely undervalued asset.

We decided that the only way we were going to gain
additional revenue from this project was to take on a partner. In the short term, this meant cutting our income in
half, but we'd actually make far more money in the long
run. We negotiated a deal with a partner to take over the
series. They would work full-time to develop the email list
and rerelease the series. By cutting my stake in the project in half, it would once again be a seven-figure income
stream for my company—and for years to come. We have
adopted this philosophy across the board. Our growth
strategy involves forming partnerships. In other words,
multiplying by dividing.

Think about it this way: How does a living cell multiply?
It multiplies by dividing. That's how life works, and look
where it's brought us.

TO ADD, SUBTRACT

James Hillman was a brilliant Jungian therapist who believed that you come to an age where you're not supposed to grow anymore, where life isn't about getting larger but going deeper. There's a biological basis for this belief, because at a certain age, growth in your body is cancer. I think there's a business parallel. Multiplying by dividing is a great strategy for growth, but you'll reach a point where your business matures. That's the time to go deep, to eliminate partnerships and capture more revenue by developing your own capabilities. You've reached the stage where it's not about growth, but depth.

Here's an example: You can capture new business territory by starting a partnership, and then you can occupy it by finishing the partnership. We partnered with Agora Financial to make a docuseries called *Wealth Breakthroughs*, a new territory for us. They paid for the film and they released it; after their costs were covered, we split the revenue. Their focus was the first and most profitable pass through the market, but we were playing a longer game. We structured the deal so that rights to the footage and the email list the series generated went to us at a certain point. The asset was ours and it was paid for, leaving us free to leverage it for more revenue going forward.

TO SPEED UP, SLOW DOWN

Embracing paradox is not only a key to business success. It applies to your well-being, too, and that needs to be part of your mindset. I've worked out all my life, and five or six years ago I finally realized that it was time for me to stop training like a high school football player. That's not my goal anymore. So, my mountain biking has turned into hiking. The weights I used to lift to warm up are now my workout weights. I used to be all about fitness and managing my weight. Now I apply a new filter to my workout choices: longevity. In my forties, longevity wasn't anywhere on my radar. But now I'm in my sixties. Slowing down my workouts keeps my workouts moving fast.

THE BOTTOM LINE:
LEAN INTO UNCERTAINTY

To embrace paradox is to recognize that there are no certainties in business, only certainties in the moment. This requires leaving the comfort of certainty behind, discarded like a pair of training wheels. How do you know when to proceed and when to turn back? When to hire or fire? When to expand or contract? When to take on a competitor or partner with them? Later in the book I'll talk about how to choose the right tool, the right strategy, in the right moment. For now, the assignment is to accept that most of your business experience will contradict itself over and over. Say goodbye to knowing you're right, and hello to brilliant, resilient flexibility.

3

SURVIVAL

It's not just can we but should we.

(FROM DAVID NEMELKA)

A lot of stories get written about entrepreneurs' bravery and foresight, but you rarely hear about their anguish. Picture this: You're alone in your office on a Wednesday and payday is Friday. You don't have the money to make payroll, but you can't share this information with your employees or they'll start looking for new jobs. Even though you've got nowhere to turn, you can't hide in your office, curled up in a fetal position. You've got to keep a smile on your face, projecting the confidence that everything is going to be fine.

At this point, many entrepreneurs double down. To keep their business alive, they'll pour everything they have into it: their income, their savings, their home equity, and their blood, sweat, and tears. They built their businesses because they wanted them to produce income and serve them, but now they're serving their businesses. What started as a business concern has now become a matter of survival.

To avoid getting into this scenario, it's important that you prioritize taking care of yourself.

I'm not the first entrepreneur to come to this realization. After James Altucher went broke for the sixth time in 2008 (and by "went broke" I mean making millions of dollars and losing it all, as I discussed in the Introduction), he finally woke up to the fact that he had a problem and needed to solve it. First, he needed to identify the problem. To that end he listed the common elements that were present when he succeeded and the common elements when he went broke. Doing this, he figured out that every time he failed, he hadn't been taking care of his "four bodies": his physical, mental, emotional, and spiritual states. After making their care a focus of his life and an integral part of his daily routine, he stopped going broke.

James explained his new philosophy to me on more than one occasion, but his advice always went right past me. "I'll get my four bodies in order," I'd assure him, before pumping him for tactical advice. "Now tell me the real secret of your success." It took me a while to realize that he was being sincere and to see the wisdom in his message.

Early in my career, I ran a company that sold water softeners door-to-door. As in any sales venture, we'd have good weeks and bad weeks. String together a few bad weeks, and it's called a slump. In the midst of one of those stretches, I called my regional manager: "Man, I don't know what to do," I said. "I'm working like crazy on closing deals, I'm working on getting more prospects in the door, I'm working on everything I can."

I wasn't expecting the answer he gave me: "Is your office clean?" I was stunned. "When I get in a slump," he continued, "I make sure the trash cans are empty. I make sure the office is spick-and-span."

It was the stupidest advice I'd ever heard, but I did it—and it worked. I was like a baseball player who'd found a pair of lucky socks. I've watched it work over and over again in the years since. Perhaps it's the placebo effect, but I think there's something mystical about the power in shifting your focus from a problem you can't solve to something else in your life that you can.

It's not just a key to success, but a key to survival. We've all been raised on hero stories, and as entrepreneurs we tend toward heroic effort. We forget what happens to the hero in our myths: the hero dies.

I spent the first half of my career heroically bursting through doors. Not anymore. Now I think of going through every door that opens. I no longer base my business—or my life—on the heroic model. Instead I think of a flow state; I know I'm in flow when things are coming easily. I try to approach my business with ease, grace, and the confidence to spend an evening cleaning my office instead of slaving over new high-pressure sales tactics. You'll be happier and more successful too. The secret to doing this well involves managing yourself and your money.

SELF-MANAGEMENT

Be Honest with Yourself

Consider Buddhism's Noble Eightfold Path—comprising the path to liberation. One of those eight cogs, right view, involves seeing the world and yourself as they truly are. As an entrepreneur, you're going to experience as much failure as you will success. I try to be honest with myself during the hard times. I try to guard against my own weaknesses and self-deception. The quicker you recognize your faults, the sooner you can address them—or cut your losses and move on. Both ways lead to progress.

People tend to compare their back stages (what's behind the scenes) with other people's front stages (what everyone can see). This tendency is exacerbated by social media, where everyone appears to be perennially on vacation or celebrating some great milestone. In today's world, it's easy to think that everyone else is succeeding and drowning in money, and you're the only one having trouble. I've learned that's not the case. We all have fears and tragedies we're forced to deal with.

This hit home for me during a Genius Network event one year. The speaker, Dr. Sean Stephenson, was a best-selling author who had been born with a rare disorder that made his bones extremely fragile. He'd had more than two hundred broken bones by the time he was eighteen and was only two-and-a-half feet tall. Most people with this condition don't live beyond their early twenties. He was forty when, in 2019, his wheelchair fell on top of him. He died a few days later. Despite these challenges, he lived a remarkable and brave life. "This is happening for me, not to me," was his mantra.

During this event, Stephenson revealed his deepest, darkest fear: his wife would be out hiking and meet someone whose body could do all the things that Stephenson's body couldn't, and she would leave him. So, he attached the hydration pack she used for hiking to his wheelchair. When she asked to borrow it, he'd say it was the only one that fit the connection to his chair. If he could hijack her CamelBak, maybe he'd stop her from hiking, meeting someone fit and attractive, and leaving him. Maybe he'd prevent his deepest fear from coming true. One day he had a hard talk with himself and faced that fear. After all, there was an REI store down the street. She could just buy another CamelBak. Then he had a talk with her and confessed what he'd done. Such honesty. It was the most poignant moment of the weekend.

Next, Sean passed out slips of paper and told us to write down our deepest, darkest secrets without including our names. He had them typed up on a single piece of paper, a copy of which we received at the end of the day. I was surrounded by forty of the most successful entrepreneurs in the country. Most of them were riddled with uncertainty and fear. "I feel like I'm a fraud" was a common response. "I'm not smart enough to be doing what I'm doing" was another. "I invested in what turned to be a Ponzi scheme, and I'm down to $20,000 in the world," said a third. "I've lost my whole fortune, and no one knows."

That's why you shouldn't compare your back stage with other people's front stage. We all suffer from our own brand of fear, even though it's easy in the middle of a storm to think you're the only one. In these dark times, I find solace in a line based on a quote from Joseph Campbell: "The cave you fear to enter holds the treasure you seek."

Surround Yourself with Successful People

There will always be people who will happily tell you that whatever you're excited about doing next is impossible. People who are eager to tell you why your idea is stupid or why it can't be done. We have to protect our mind from these people, insulate ourselves from them, and have a plan in place. My plan is to surround myself with people who do what other people say is impossible.

Our friends and colleagues have an even greater influence on us than our parents because of the role that mirror neurons play in our conditioning. The mirror neurons in our brains fire whenever we observe someone else doing something. When this happens, we feel like we've actually done it ourselves.

This finding is profoundly important for addicts. When people are addicted to opiates, the part of their brain that would restrict overuse becomes damaged. It's the answer to the question, why can't you stop your self-destructive behavior? It explains that, when you put addicts together with people who are navigating life without opiates, they don't just see other people doing it—they feel as if they have done it themselves. A new environment can lead to progress, and that's the work of mirror neurons.

That's why I spend $170,000 a year attending mastermind events, like the Genius Network event where we all revealed our deepest fears. I always learn tactical things at these events, but the most important thing I take away is seeing how to play the entrepreneurial game at a higher level. By the end of the morning on the first day, I'm always struck by the same epiphany: I'm thinking too small. Like many entrepreneurs, I get stuck in the same hole as everybody else in my business. We can't see outside it. Going to mastermind events helps me climb out of the hole.

Mastermind events are also where I charge my batteries in the company of other entrepreneurs like me. I've found it's not something I can do with my team. It's no different than women recharging their femininity in the company of other women, while men recharge their masculinity in the company of other men. In a personal relationship, I bring my masculine energy to my partner and she brings her feminine energy to me—but I don't recharge my masculinity in her company. That's why there are men's groups. And that's why, in the company of other entrepreneurs, I can best recharge my spirit, my ambition, my drive, my thinking, my ability to lead.

Find a Mentor

For entrepreneurs, having a mentor is essential. So, how should one go about establishing such a relationship? It's not a formalized process. You don't walk up to someone you respect and ask, "Hey, would you be my mentor?" I've had many mentors, and perhaps none ever realized they were playing that role for me. Mentors are friends who evolve into something more than that. The more relationships you develop, the more mentors you'll find. They make all the difference. You need someone outside of your company you can call and tell the absolute truth to, so they can point you in the right direction. They won't have the same stress you're feeling at that moment, but they've surely felt it in the past.

"I won't do for you what you should do for yourself," David Nemelka used to tell me, "but you can lean on me during a storm."

I can't count the number of times I did that over the years, just as I can't begin to calculate how valuable his guidance was to me, in business and in my personal life.

Imagine how different the story of Enron—or any other corporate business scandal—might have been if someone at the top had leaned on a mentor of David's quality. He'd have told them what he told me, many times: "It's not just, 'Can we do it?' It's, 'Should we do it?'"

Avoid Time Sucks

At one point in my career I had a lot of success with crowdfunding, and I was getting bombarded by people calling to ask if they could pick my brain for a minute. "I want to do some crowdfunding," they'd say. "Can I take you to lunch and get your feedback?"

I was getting about ten of these calls a week. Trying to be kind, I helped these people as much as possible until a friend set me straight: "The worst thing an entrepreneur can do is get involved in things that take time but don't make money."

In 2019, the entrepreneur Joel Marion hosted a mastermind event that grossed $10 million, but he told me it wasn't profitable because he spent more than $10 million of his time creating it. What struck me most was that he knew the exact value of his time and used it to figure out if the event was a success. Joel isn't someone you email unless you have something important to say, and even then it had better be short. He knows the exact value of his time, and he spends it wisely.

I've learned a lot from him. Now when somebody asks me for an hour of my time, I ask myself, "Is spending an hour with this person worth $1,000 to me?" Or if I have to drive thirty minutes to meet someone and thirty minutes back, "Is it worth a couple thousand dollars to have lunch with this guy just so he can ask me a favor?"

Expect to Be Fired

William Durant was a quintessential entrepreneur whose life illustrates all the glories and pitfalls that await us. A high school dropout, he made a fortune building horse-drawn carriages, then went on to take control of the Buick Motor Company in 1904. Instead of putting all its energy into making a single type of car, such as Ford's Model T, Buick produced a variety of cars and, following Durant's orders, acquired a string of thirty companies, including Cadillac, Oakland, and Oldsmobile, under the overarching corporate umbrella of General Motors. His expansionist mindset proved costly. In 1911, the company's board of directors forced Durant to quit.

Undeterred, Durant founded a new car company, Chevrolet, which became so successful so quickly he was able to buy enough General Motors stock to regain control of the company in 1916. Unfortunately, his stance against the United States' participation in World War I, combined with a growing gambling addiction, led to his professional demise, and he was forced out once again in 1920. During the Depression, he went bankrupt, and he spent the last years of his life managing a bowling alley in Flint, Michigan. Once a titan of wealth, William Durant died poor and has been lost to history.

The story of Durant's colleague Alfred P. Sloan has a happier ending. Sloan was the CEO of General Motors, a man with a very different skill set than Durant that made him well suited to run the company. Sloan died a staggeringly wealthy man, and his legacy lives on. The Memorial Sloan Kettering Cancer Center? The MIT Sloan School of Management? Both took their names from Alfred P. Sloan.

The story of a visionary entrepreneur dying broke is all too common in the business world. Every time I've started a company that gets big, sooner or later I'm brought in for a "Durant meeting," where I'm told: "This company is amazing. You did such a great job. We could not be where we are without you. But it's grown too big for you, and we need to bring in some professional managers."

That's a nice way of saying, "You're fired."

The most important thing you can do is to plan for this moment and not be surprised when it comes. It's inevitable. If your idea is brilliant, it will be harvested. For any business that's growing, replacing the visionary founder with an experienced management team is a natural step. Instead of seeing this as a moment of failure, I interpret it as a moment of success. The dream I once had is now solid enough to stand on its own. I'm on to my next dream, and I don't look back.

DAVID'S WISDOM
NEGOTIATING WITH HIS OWN BRAIN

The entrepreneurial life can be so exciting, and it's not always easy to be present with your kids.

David managed this by negotiating with his own brain. They'd make a deal: "If you will let me be fully present and fully engaged here with my son or my daughter, then tonight at eight o'clock, I will do nothing but think about business for two solid hours."

David's brain drove a hard bargain—but his kids were the beneficiaries. And that's a win-win.

MONEY MANAGEMENT

Establishing Your Nonnegotiables

I've learned—the hard way—the importance of defining my nonnegotiables before I start a business. Banks and investors will offer you loans or investments that require a personal guarantee, and I've found that, long before that happens, I need to have decided what my response will be. Is this a risk I'm willing to take if the payoff is right? Or is this a line in the sand I'm unwilling to cross, a hard stance I consider nonnegotiable? I decide my position on personal guarantees long before they are ever presented to me. If you don't and you're in desperate need of capital for your company, and a loan you're offered requires a personal guarantee, you're going to take it.

Many of my business friends consider personal guarantees to be a nonnegotiable. No matter how badly their company might need the money, they will never risk their personal fortunes.

The pro football coach Cam Cameron once told me about a meeting he had with the owner, the general manager, and the head coach of an NFL team that had just hired him to be its offensive coordinator. The team had a problem, and the only solution that had been proposed was unethical. During an upcoming meeting with the league, they were going to have to say some things that weren't true. As he was telling me this story, I thought he was going to tell me about the dilemma he faced: whether or not to go along with the team's plan. But for him it wasn't a dilemma at all, because he already had his nonnegotiables in place. He lived by a very firm code of ethics. So, if the team required him to go along with its plan, he was perfectly happy to sell the house he'd just bought and move across the country with his wife to work for another team. In the end, he proposed a way to handle the situation that wouldn't require them to lie, and the team decided to do it that way.

One of my biggest nonnegotiables is always paying my Form 941 payroll tax withholding the second I get it. If one of my businesses doesn't have the capital to make payroll and pay the payroll tax, I shut the business down. I came to realize the importance of this the hard way.

I once owned a telemarketing company that was growing incredibly slowly. During its first year, we did $10 million in revenue, but we only made 2 or 3 percent profit. That's like flying a 747 just above the treetops. At that level, your engine will suck up a tree every now and then, and the plane will crash. Often, we'd barely make payroll and there wouldn't be enough money left over to make our 941 deposit. Other times, we'd set aside the 941 tax money and then we'd be short on payroll two weeks later and have to raid the tax account to make payroll. We were constantly kicking the can down the road, and at the end of that company's second year, its 941 account was $2 million in debt.

Fortunately, I was able to sell the business for more than $2 million, making a slight profit—or so I thought. The company I sold the business to gave me a chunk of money up front and agreed to pay off the 941 debt within six months. Unfortunately, that company went broke and didn't pay it off, and the IRS informed me that the contract I'd signed with the company that had purchased the debt meant nothing. When it comes to 941 taxes, you can't hide behind a corporate veil.

Suddenly, I had a $2 million tax lien from a business that I didn't even own, and I had to pay it out of personal income. Now whenever I look at a business that needs help or one I might buy, the first thing I do is check the status of its payroll tax account.

Profit First

The normal math for running a business is revenue minus expense equals profit. The problem with this equation is that making a profit is actually an unnatural state for a company because businesses tend to absorb all available income. We're taught that the purpose of a business is to make a profit, but unless you intervene, a business will always absorb 100 percent of the capital available to it, and it will never make a profit. In companies that are making lots of revenue, the expenses grow just as fast and absorb it all. New employees get hired, systems get automated, managers get brought in, and the company is left hovering around the break-even point.

To combat this, my business partner Patrick Gentempo and I adopted a strategy from entrepreneur Mike Michalowicz called Profit First: revenue − profit = expenses. We decide on the percentage we're hoping to grow each year, and that becomes our profit margin. We pull that money out and put it in an entirely different bank and run the company using whatever money's left over. That account determines whether we can afford to hire a new person or buy new cameras or not. Had I followed this business model at the beginning of my career, I would have safeguarded millions of dollars. Instead I ended up pouring that money into various businesses that absorbed it all.

Building Your Income Before Your Business
One of the best pieces of advice I can give young entrepreneurs is to build your income before you build your business. It doesn't matter where that income originates. I know people who have done it by buying income-generating real estate, and others who've done it by buying a car wash.

My friend the entrepreneur Naomi Whittel once told me that, in her early twenties, she determined that she needed $3,500 to live on each month. Once she succeeded in reaching that income, thanks to her real estate savvy, she was free to take some chances in business. In 2009, she started a company called Reserveage Nutrition that sold nutritional supplements, and six years later she sold it for $37 million. She put that money into income-producing bonds and the interest from those bonds now covers her substantially larger monthly nut. She is a risk-taking entrepreneur, but she has never risked her own money, because she always builds her income before her businesses.

Keeping a Personal War Chest

I once made three documentary films in a row that didn't do well, and I ended up carrying way too much debt. But I had a project coming to fruition that had the potential to bring in enough money to wipe out all my debt and generate a little profit.

"What are you going to do with the money this deal brings in?" my business coach asked me.

I thought I was being smart when I said, "The first thing I want to do is get rid of all this debt."

"No way," he said. "You're going to have to do another project to wipe out your debt. The first thing you must do is set aside a war chest. Because war will come again, and if you don't have a war chest, it'll take you down."

For me, that number was $300,000. This is not income-producing money. This is not money to buy real estate. This is a war chest: money you've set aside to deal with the crap that's sure to come your way. If you're investing in real estate and don't have the money to pay for a new roof or manage the months when you're not getting rent, don't buy the property.

"You've got to be able to sleep when the wind blows," David Nemelka once told me. If you don't have a war chest, you'll never sleep.

On to the Wealth Account

It took me a long time to recognize that the very skills that make a successful entrepreneur are devastating to building long-term wealth. The biggest asset for an entrepreneur is the willingness to take risks, but if you're constantly taking risks with your wealth, you will eventually lose it. Once I establish a steady income for myself and fill my war chest, I build my wealth account. This money has nothing to do with my latest ideas or building my newest business. It's there to grow my long-term wealth.

Patrick Byrne, the CEO of Overstock, became a protégé of Warren Buffett at age thirteen. He built a sizable fortune even before he'd founded Overstock, and Buffett's advice was telling: You never need to take a risk, because you're already wealthy. Sit and wait for the perfect pitch before swinging your bat.

Great advice. It goes against every instinct of the entrepreneurial brain. We often swing at every pitch we see, and we're excited to do it. The path to long-term survival awaits those who master their instincts.

4

PRACTICALLY DELUSIONAL

The leader never gets off the hot seat. Once you
accept that, start to turn up the heat.

(FROM LOWELL FOLETTA)

In my late twenties, I was a stockbroker along with my two
best friends, Jim Rennert and Red McMillan. We would
often talk about what we wanted to do with our lives,
because all three of us knew we weren't put on this earth to
be stockbrokers.

"I want to be a sculptor," said Jim.

"I want to be a pilot," said Red.

"I want to be a filmmaker," I said.

"How do you make a film?" they asked.

"I don't have a clue," I confessed. "But I see them all the
time, so somebody knows how to make them."

If anybody overheard these three twentysomething
stockbrokers, two of whom were high school dropouts,
discussing their dreams, they would have told us we were

delusional. Fortunately, we were "practically delusional," the term I've coined to describe how important it is for those of us with entrepreneurial brains to be practical at the same time we're delusional. We need to be aware of our tendencies and put some filters in place to stop ourselves from driving off cliffs in pursuit of our dreams. But that's not to say we should—or even could—stop ourselves from dreaming.

We were unlikely candidates to get our dream jobs. A former wrestler at Brigham Young University, Jim was artistic, but I never envisioned him making a living as a sculptor. Now he is featured in his own art gallery at Fifty-Seventh and Fifth in New York City. His sculptures have been displayed in the National Gallery of Art and sell for as much as $400,000. Like me, Red was a high school dropout, but he's now the chief pilot at Spirit Airlines. And I've made close to twenty documentary films, one of which was short-listed for an Academy Award.

MY DELUSIONAL LEAP

While watching Michael Moore's documentary *Fahrenheit 9/11* after it was released in May 2004, I thought it was seriously flawed. It was clear that Moore had manipulated interviews as he tried to hammer home his message, and the film attempted to make two conflicting points: President George Bush was a blundering idiot, and at the same time a grand wizard at the head of a massive conspiracy making trillions of dollars for the oil companies.

The Republican Party did the strategically smart thing, which was to ignore it. Normally, documentaries play to very small audiences and usually make less than $5 million at the box office. But Moore got hold of great footage, and he knew what to do with it. He'd show Bush making what seemed like a serious statement, then turning around to hit a golf ball. *Fahrenheit 9/11* made $100 million right out of the gate and would go on to gross $222 million, making it the most successful documentary ever made. It had a huge impact on our culture—and it caught Republicans flat-footed. This left a vacuum, and it occurred to me to fill the void with a counter-documentary.

I knew it was a smart move with a huge chance of succeeding. But self-doubt crept in. I vacillated for almost a month. "What gives me the right to make this film?" I thought. "Out of all the people in the world, why should I be the one to make a rebuttal film to the most successful documentary of all time? What in the world is wrong with my brain that I think I could do this?" I wasn't politically active. The Republican Party didn't even know my name. I'd never made a documentary before, and I was proposing to go head-to-head with the most successful documentary filmmaker in history.

It was delusional to think I could do this.

But in reality, it was *practically* delusional. I could call on contacts, tap into relationships—and I knew the steps needed to get it done. I didn't know anyone in politics, but I knew which gatekeeper I needed: Dick Morris, Bill Clinton's chief political advisor turned contributor to Fox News. I reached out through his agent and solidified the deal with money.

I made more calls and assembled a team and a director. We started filming on August 19, 2004, in New York. We interviewed Morris, who also connected us with the former mayor of New York Ed Koch, the US senator from Georgia Zell Miller, and the conservative media pundit Ann Coulter.

We worked around the clock. Editors slept in sleeping bags in the office. From start to finish, we managed to make the film in twenty-eight days, meeting the deadline we needed to match the release date of Moore's DVD. We titled it *Fahrenhype 9/11,* so our DVD would sit right next to Moore's on the shelves at Blockbuster. I'd done it!

That's where the entrepreneur's delusion can lead you. It is what Steve Jobs was referring to when he said, "Here's to the crazy ones, the misfits, the rebels, the troublemakers, the round pegs in the square holes, the ones who see things differently." We look at things that everyone else thinks of as impossible, and something in our brains says, "No, we can do this." But if we can't temper that impulse—making ourselves *practically* delusional—we become our own worst enemies.

CROSSING THE LINE

There's a fine line between being practically delusional and just plain delusional. The key is to be aware of our tendency to tilt at windmills. We need to put filters in place to check our behavior.

A few years ago, another would-be filmmaker asked to meet with me. He told me he had a brilliant idea for a film; he was certain it was going to make $100 million.

"What's the budget for the film?" I asked.

"Ten million dollars," he said.

"How are you going to finance it?"

He was going to get a big-name Hollywood actor like Tom Cruise to commit to playing the lead role, which would allow him to raise the $10 million he needed to make the film. This idea would only make sense to somebody who didn't know the film business.

I explained to him that his idea was a good one, but its time was past. People in Hollywood have tried to get projects off the ground using an A-list actor's name to raise money for a spec project thousands of times, and it was no longer possible. Agents know the precise value of their clients' names, and they're not interested in letting them be used for free so that some entrepreneur can make money. If you want to sign Tom Cruise, you have to sign a pay-or-play deal, which guarantees that he'll be paid his enormous fee, regardless of whether your film actually gets made.

When I explained all this, my visitor lost it, telling me that he couldn't wait until he made his film so he could shove it in my face. It hasn't happened yet. He had crossed the line from practically delusional to just plain delusional.

It's not a good place to be—and you don't have to go there.

CHECKING YOUR VALUES

I've kept a journal for a long time, and at some point along the way I realized that in writing my entries I was revealing my values. I don't mean aspirational, Ben Franklin values like integrity and thrift. I'm talking about the operating values that guide your decisions, whether or not you're aware of them. Everyone has them; they're built in, and they're running in the background all the time. I set aside a page, and as I wrote my journal entries I began to list the values my day-to-day decisions revealed. In a month, I'd amassed a list that seemed to encompass the values I lived by. It was a journey into self-awareness. For one thing, I probably value humor a lot more than most people. Not all my values were consistent, and some were in tension. So, I ranked them: I value comfort, money, and relationships. But because I value comfort over money, I'm happy to pay for a first-class ticket if I don't get upgraded for free. I value relationships more than I value money too. I value them both—but given the choice, I would choose relationships.

Where does this lead? How does it help me separate delusion from practical delusion?

I've found that when I have problems with people in the business world, it's often because they value money more than relationships. When push comes to shove, they'll make decisions that surprise me.

This sort of mismatch in values is guaranteed to destroy a partnership. Before I commit to a new project, I evaluate the values of my proposed partners. If they don't align with mine, I either avoid them or the project. It's not that they're in the wrong. Their values and mine simply don't match. You can think of marriage the same way. If you value entrepreneurship and risk-taking, and your spouse values stability and security, you're destined for trouble.

Simplicity, Probability, and Leverage

I like new things. I like complicated things. But before I launch, buy, or invest in a business, I run it through a filter

I borrowed from the well-known business consultant Rick Sapio. I've learned to measure my latest delusion by three values: simplicity, probability, and leverage. When I heard Rick list them, I recognized them immediately— because I had violated them more than once. I've done complex businesses. I've done low-probability businesses. I've wasted my time in ventures that didn't have any leverage. In fact, I once combined all three in one venture.

During the 1990s, a business associate of mine was brought in to run Piper Aircraft while it was in bankruptcy. Though Piper was profitable, the company was being dragged down by liability risks that involved private planes that were still flying as long as a half-century after the company built them. Congress had recognized this as a problem and planned to address it by changing liability law for private aircraft manufacturers.

My associate called to ask if I'd put up $500,000 to buy the company. I did—with four partners, we bought Piper while it was still in bankruptcy. We petitioned Congress to change the liability law and prepared for takeoff.

The good news is that Congress changed the law. The bad news is that it took ten years. By then the bankruptcy had been finalized, wiping out all of our equity.

Now I know better.

Simplicity always wins over complexity. This filter will take you out of some deals, and I'm willing to accept that. Before the financial crash of 2008, people were making fortunes in Wall Street derivatives. They're far from simple. Complexity's not necessarily wrong, but it's not for me. I value business opportunities that are easy to understand. I value simplicity.

Probability measures the likelihood of success. You can do it up front. A group of ten billionaires funded a company called Planetary Resources in hopes of capturing an asteroid and mining its minerals. I'm sure these guys don't look at it as a high-probability venture, but to them, it's worth attempting. It's nothing I'd want to bet my career on—after all, none of the billionaires are. They're at the stage in life where they can take flyers on fascinating deals. Not me. Right now, I value opportunities that are high probability.

To me, leverage is an even higher value than simplicity and probability. Does a project utilize my existing assets, my relationships, and my skill set to create something that's not there? Not long ago I bought a ten-thousand-square-foot soundstage and recording studio in Utah. I posted photos on Facebook and immediately heard from Facebook friends: love to rent that soundstage! I passed. I had zero interest in renting it out even when I wasn't using it. Renting space is a service business that feels like a job to me and, at a few hundred dollars an hour, offers nothing in the way of leverage. Filming my documentaries there does. When I use the stage and the studio to make and release a documentary, I can make millions of dollars. I value leverage.

Again, there's no absolute right or wrong here. It's about what's right or wrong for you and for your potential partners. But I will add this: if your business venture requires an act of Congress and takes you into an arena where you've got zero experience to begin with . . . let's just say that's the opposite of simplicity, probability, and leverage.

DAVID'S DELUSION
ORGAN DONATIONS

David Nemelka was nothing if not practically delusional. I got a call from him once asking me to join him for a meeting. It was with the leaders of the organ donor association in Utah. We met in their boardroom.

"Why are people dying every day for lack of organs?" David asked the leaders. "We're burying people every day with organs that can be used. What are the obstacles?"

The leaders cited several issues, two of which have stuck in my mind. Even though people could check a box when they got their license signifying that they would be an organ donor, at the time of death the state of Utah still required approval from the next of kin. In that moment of grief, sadness, and shock, the next of kin frequently declined. The would-be donor's wishes were not being upheld. Fixing that would require a change in state law.

A second issue was Mormon lore. The widespread belief among Mormons was that they were to return their body to God intact. In fact, this was never a doctrine of the church. *The General Handbook*, to which local Mormon ward leaders look for guidance, was silent on the issue of organ donation. Fixing that would require a change in the handbook, a process almost as difficult as amending the US Constitution.

But people were dying. David couldn't tolerate the thought of it. He reached into his pocket and pulled out a check. "Here's a $25,000 donation," he said, "and it's the first of many. I will help you solve these problems." Then he pounded the table and boomed out his next words. (David did not have an inside voice.) "But listen to me!" he said. "If you take my money, I have a right to speak. If you're not going to listen to me, don't take my money." He was giving value in the form of a donation, and seeking value in the form of a role in their work to change laws.

They took the money. They listened to David. And things changed. Within two years, *The General Handbook* had been modified in support of organ donations. The law in Utah got changed, too, and David worked with the state to set up a website called "Yes Utah" where would-be donors could bypass the next of kin rule if they signed up online. The governor and his wife were the first two people to do it.

Utah went from a 30 percent rate of organ donors to 70 percent, leading the nation.

ANSWERING YOUR OWN QUESTIONS

The easiest way to fall into delusion is self-validating your own ideas. This occurs in every arena, not just business. When we live inside our own idea, or validate our idea only with those who already share it, we're not building a business. We're creating a cult, because we're not exposing our idea to the test of reality. Entrepreneurs are generally so enthusiastic and persuasive that we risk looking for approval by gathering people who will tell us only what we want to hear.

Twenty-five years ago, I was a runner. I'm flat-footed, and I developed shin splints and stress fractures in both legs. But I was determined to keep running. When I went to a doctor who advised me to stop running, I decided what I really needed was a different doctor. And so, of course, I went to doctor after doctor until I found ones who told me what I needed were an anti-inflammatory and a new orthotic. I discounted all the good advice I was getting from doctors who said that, given my build, I should look for a new activity. Finding doctors who would validate my false reality didn't change the fact that I could no longer run. Now I'm a hiker, and I'm happier and healthier too.

It's easy to be defensive in the face of criticism, to turn away from things you don't want to hear. It's much more fun to seek attaboys and validation. So, to protect myself from self-delusion, I've learned to set aside my desire to sell, to persuade, and instead to seek and really consider hard feedback on my ideas.

Validating with Smart People

It's okay to put your idea in front of people just for the sheer joy of sharing—to demonstrate to yourself once again that you can pitch the crap out of anything and leave your audience loving it.

But that's entirely different than seeking to validate your concept with smart people. I've learned that getting the hard and useful feedback I need begins with learning who to talk with. Some people love to pick your ideas apart, out of cynicism or jealousy. That's not what I'm talking about. What I've learned to look for are thoughtful, experienced people who ask probing questions and may have traveled some sections of the road I'm describing.

I once had a business partner tell me that every idea has to survive the hot anvil of debate. It's one of the reasons it's great to develop relationships with private equity firms and venture capitalists. (I'll talk about how to do that later in the book.) You can go to them when you're looking not for money, but validation. That's their job, their livelihood. They're fascinated by new ideas, and they're the quickest thinkers I've ever met. It doesn't take them long to poke holes in a bad idea. I've learned to fight the instinct to parry their objections, like a lawyer in a courtroom; it's far more useful to listen.

We've all got mentors in life we can draw on, whether they wear that label or not. It could be someone you work with, someone you mountain bike with, a peer. They may simply know one more chapter of the book than you do—and they also know you. Some mentors are best suited to banging your idea on that hot anvil of debate. Others are great at evaluating your idea in the context of what they know about *you*. These are the people who ask the questions that shine a light into the unexplored corners of your thinking, and who know you well enough to call bullshit when they hear it.

Asking for feedback has value beyond validation. It suggests humility and openness, and it's a great way to develop relationships. A vice president in one of my companies excelled at this. Whenever we had a new idea, he'd set up five or six meetings with people, and he'd ask them for their advice about a project. "I know you know a lot more about this than I do. What do you think? Where are we wrong here?" He was so earnest and so sincere that people would counsel him for hours and hours. He came away with insights into the strengths and weaknesses of his idea—and he built relationships too.

I've learned to work my contact list. If my idea is in a new field, I ask my contacts if they know anyone who's done anything like it. I've also learned that when others help me, I need to help others in return. If someone calls me and wants to talk about nuclear technology, I'm not going to take the meeting, because I have no expertise in the area. But if someone calls me and says, "My son has written a film script, and he's looking for advice from someone in the industry," I'll take the meeting. When I give, I get. I've seen it happen time and again.

Validating with Customers

During the first internet boom, Webvan, an online company that promised to deliver groceries to your door in thirty minutes, raised more than $396 million from venture capitalists and $375 million more from an initial public offering. Over the next three years, the company spent more than $525 million building warehouses all around the country and buying a fleet of delivery trucks.

It was an era when ideas were everything, treasured and valued so highly that start-ups raised and spent millions in stealth mode. And by today's standards of lifestyle, Webvan's model *does* seem like a great idea. But they were twenty years ahead of their time. They failed to validate their idea with consumers, and the results were disastrous. People weren't ready to buy groceries on the internet. Webvan lost more than $800 million and filed for bankruptcy in 2001.

It was a perfect example of hubris. It's like the old joke about the dog food company. The sales reps loved the dog food, and the scientists loved the dog food, and everything just seemed great about the dog food. "If all this is true," the president said one day, "why are we doing so bad?"

A hand went up in the back. "Well, sir," a sales rep said, "the dogs don't like it."

I've been there. I've built businesses that I loved and my team loved and my investors loved. But the customers didn't want it.

One of the best concepts to emerge from the rubble of that first internet crash was the minimum viable product, or MVP. It's part of a software development technique called Agile that emphasizes launching a new product as quickly as possible and with only enough features to satisfy early adopters, validating the promise in your idea—or the lack of it—as early as possible and at minimal cost, while guiding you toward your next step. The origins of Agile software development and the associated Scrum method for organizing the work can be traced to the 1990s.

With Agile software development, you create the simplest viable version of software and get it out as soon as possible. You typically work in one-, two-, or at most four-week increments, or Scrums, and you're constantly getting feedback from customers, incorporating it, and releasing updated versions of the product. This is how Google and Facebook were built. Many companies now release new additions to their software every day.

The concept of MVP works for entrepreneurs too. It's the ultimate validation of our ideas and the best path to success, because it is customers who drive it through their behavior.

There's a worse way to seek validation from customers: the survey. Surveys mean nothing. For years fast-food companies used surveys to solicit feedback from their customers, and the people who filled them out would always claim they wanted "low-calorie, healthy fast food." The companies would respond by rolling out this sort of food in all their stores across the country, and these products always failed. When people pull up to the drive-thru at a Taco Bell or McDonald's, they're looking for taste, and that means fattening, greasy fast food. We'd all be much healthier if we meant what we said in surveys, but the truth is we love fast food. And when it comes to drawing the line between delusion and practical delusion, it's learning the truth that matters.

THE *FAHRENHYPE* LESSONS

I opened this chapter by talking about *Fahrenhype 9/11*, my answer to Michael Moore's blockbuster documentary. I left off on October 6, 2004, the day we released the film. There's actually much more to the story of making the documentary than just filming it.

Back in September, Patrick Byrne, the CEO of Overstock .com, had invited me to his office to show him the film. Fifteen minutes in, he elbowed me. "You're walking out of here with an order for at least half a million dollars," he told me. We watched a little more. "Hey, this is really good," he said. "You're going to walk out of here with at least a million-dollar order." Halfway through, he asked what it would take to get an exclusive on it.

I already had a distributor, and he'd struck a deal with a third party to distribute the DVD through Walmart.

"Is your deal signed?" Patrick asked.

It wasn't, I said, but it's a deal. He countered with a million-dollar offer for the rights to online distribution—and handed me the check.

Overstock's office was in the town where I lived, and I went home to call my distributor. "You had a check for a million dollars in your hand?" he said. "What, are you an idiot? Take the money. We'll work this out; it'll be fine."

When I returned to Patrick's office, he upped the offer again. "I want to buy all the rights," he said. "I'll take over the Walmart order, and we'll give you $2.3 million." At an earlier time, I had once been wealthy, but I wasn't wealthy anymore. Patrick knew that—and so he upped his offer again. "How much do I have to pay for you to walk out the door a millionaire?" he asked. I did the math—the expenses in making the film, what my investors were due. The answer was $2.6 million.

And that's what Patrick paid me.

I tell that story to show you where practical delusion can lead.

But it's not my last Patrick story.

After *Fahrenhype 9/11*, I was eager to find another opportunity to work with Patrick. It came when he reached out to me with an idea for another political film in time for the 2016 election. It was an attack film, and it wasn't in line with my values. I like creating movements that are for, not against. But it was my chance to work again with Patrick, and I wasn't going to say no. He put up money for the film, and so did I.

Patrick's idea shouldn't have made it past my values check. But it did.

The result, a film called *Rigged 2016,* wasn't a failure from a financial point of view. But making it involved two and a half years of misery, because my heart wasn't in it. It wasn't aligned with my values. I wasn't motivated by commitment, but by obligation.

It would have been fine if my primary value was making money. It wasn't, and it isn't. I should have known better. Instead I deluded myself, and it's no one's fault but mine.

5

THE TRUE
WIN-WIN

Different is better than better.

(FROM JEFF'S NOTEBOOK)

When Stephen Covey's *The 7 Habits of Highly Effective People* came out in 1989, he injected a new phrase into the language of business: the "win-win." The book and the phrase became so popular that you couldn't even describe a business deal without at least paying lip service to it. It got so overused that when somebody came at me talking win-win, I headed for the door, because I knew I was about to hear about a deal that was in no way win-win.

But over time I've come to take the phrase seriously, as Covey intended it: not "I win and you look out for yourself," but "I win and you win." I think it's a key to survival as an entrepreneur—but only if you structure your deals in the first place to ensure it happens. It's far more common for deals to fall on one side or the other. To me the deals worth making are the deals that work to the highest good and benefit of all involved.

That's a true win–win.

My friend Scott Elder is a brilliant guy who learned that lesson the hard way. Back in the 1990s, a well-known business professor and bestselling author moved to the community where Scott lived. The professor was his hero. He reached out; they developed a business relationship. Scott was a filmmaker, and he produced and funded a DVD the professor used for promotional purposes. Before one big event, the professor placed an unusually big order of DVDs and said he would FedEx a check after. He was already behind in his payments, but Scott filled the order just the same. When the FedEx envelope arrived, it didn't contain a check, but a bankruptcy notice. The professor had front-loaded his supply of DVDs before declaring bankruptcy. When Scott called him, the professor expressed no regrets. As a business owner, the professor said, he was obligated to do what was in the best interest of his company. That, he said, was Scott's obligation as well. Sending him the DVDs without payment was a poor business decision, Scott's fault and not the professor's.

This was no small blow. It wiped Scott out. He recovered—he later founded a successful company called Investools, which ran business seminars—and never forgot the lesson he'd learned. He'd interpreted win-win to mean ensuring that the other guy won, and he'd been operating on the assumption that if his partner made out well in a deal, so would he. When he struck a deal with the professor—who clearly valued money more than relationships—he set himself up to fail.

I've been there, too, on the other side of the equation, and I'm not proud of it. When I was in my twenties, I owned a collection of companies that sold water softeners through direct sales throughout Texas, where the water's very hard. I'd built one company in Waco that had about twenty-five employees and was doing well. One person we had hired as a sales rep loved the business and wanted to own it. She had never owned a business before, but she wanted to be me. She and her husband came up with the money, and I structured a deal with them to sell her the business with money down and monthly payments.

I sold it to her for more than I was making as the owner. I remember thinking, "Wow, I'm a great negotiator." I was young and stupid. Six months later she went broke, because the deal set her up to fail. By not taking care of her interests, I injured myself. But it also taught me from that point forward, it doesn't do you any good to strike a deal that doesn't work for the other person. You end up losing, too, in the long run.

I'm now sold on a deep commitment to a win-win-win. I won't do a deal that's not structured so I win and the other party wins. That's two wins. What's the third? Everybody wins. The community benefits, because the deal serves the highest good for the benefit of all.

What's amazing is that it's always an option. And if a deal can't be structured that way, then it's not for me. I want nothing to do with a deal where I make money and my partner makes money, but the community suffers. As long as we're going to be spending our lives working on projects, they might as well be projects that benefit everyone involved.

I've developed a simple, formatted phrase for setting my business goals: "It's easier than I ever imagined to (whatever the goal is) in a win-win way for the highest good and the benefit of all involved."

I literally force all my business goals and all my business plans into this structure. It opens me to the right way of thinking. I'm expecting to be surprised and delighted with how things work out better than I ever imagined, to the benefit and highest good of everyone involved.

Imagine if that philosophy became pervasive.

SPOTTING THE WIN-LOSE

From the time I was eighteen until I turned twenty-five, most of my sales and business training came from listening to Zig Ziglar cassette tapes and going to Zig Ziglar seminars. Zig was a great salesman and motivational speaker. At the time, I was driving all over West Texas selling water softeners or siding, and on those two-hour, three-hour, five-hour road trips, it was Zig Ziglar all the time. I loved the philosophy behind Zig's signature phrase: "You can get everything in life you want if you will just help enough other people get what they want."

Then I got in the brokerage business and discovered a world that was win-lose. Not in every component, but if somebody executes a trade and makes money, there is someone on the other side who lost money. It is a harsh business, and my first exposure to a zero-sum game. If traders are talking and one of them accidentally lets something slip about a personal position they have, the other traders will pounce. It is sharks in a tank.

I realized the win-win philosophy couldn't be found anywhere. There really are businesses that are win-lose, and you can get rich acting on that philosophy. There are millionaire contractors who rely on subcontractors to build their next building. When it's time to pay the subs, they delay and delay until the subs are on the ropes. And then, when the subs are at their weakest, with employees clamoring to be paid, these contractors will negotiate a settlement for a fraction of what they'd agreed to. I've seen venture capitalists play the same game—agreeing to a term sheet and then sitting on the money as the start-up starts building. When it gets to the point that the start-up is starved for cash, the VCs will claim market conditions have changed and renegotiate the terms to their advantage.

Win-losers don't build; they take.

I'm not going to play those games. I won't do projects with people who do.

How do you avoid them? It goes back to values. Generally people will disclose their operating values, whether they're aware of them or not. I've learned to look for one clue that's strange: their office. For people who put money first, their office is meaningless. I've seen guys who are worth a hundred million dollars rotate their office from one place to the next; they're not going to waste money that can be pulled out of their business. As a general rule, I've found that people who love their work tend to invest in the place where they do that work.

Here's a second tell: The potential partner who says, "Jeff, this is a way for us to make money for our families, and isn't that what it's about for all of us?" That's his highest operating value. It's not wrong. I want to take money home for my family too. But it's not all I'm playing for; I want to add value to the world, creating new things that delight people.

In the end, of course, it all comes down to the contract. Oftentimes I've had people say: "I realize this isn't what we talked about. That's just my lawyer. He makes me say this stuff, but it's not what we'll really do."

Never sign an agreement when what's in the document doesn't capture the deal you've agreed to. When someone asks you to sign something you didn't agree to, the answer is, "Tell you what—let's write down exactly what we said." If it's not win-win in the document, it's not going to be win-win in practice.

THE DISEASE OF MORE

One of the enemies of a true win-win structure is the disease of more. When I was in my early thirties, I made an investment that gave me twenty-five hours a month in a Learjet 24, which is like a flying cigar tube. It's wonderful but it's small. There's no bathroom; you can't stand up in it. Once when I flew into the private plane terminal in Salt Lake City, I looked out the window at the plane next to us—a Gulfstream 3. At the time, the G3s were the biggest that Gulfstream made.

I walked into the terminal and asked, "Who owns that plane out there?" It was a local billionaire named Jon Huntsman, although I had never heard of him. I said, "Well, what did he do?"

Remember when McDonald's Big Macs and Quarter Pounders came in a Styrofoam container? He owned Huntsman Corporation, which made all those containers—and much more. His jet was still there when we left the next day. I sat in the Learjet feeling poor because there was a much bigger plane that I couldn't afford. Imagine sitting in a Learjet and feeling poor; something was definitely wrong.

That's the disease of more. If you have it, you'll never be happy.

A friend of mine, Dave Blanchard, wrote a book titled *More, Then Enough.* I love his title—an interesting and wise play on words. Dave makes the case that before we launch our career, we need to decide how much. At what point do we call it a win? At what point are we working for something other than money? How much is enough? Then you focus on more—until it's enough. It doesn't mean that you reach enough and quit. It means you reach enough and then you can do vastly different things with your money beyond stacking it in a pile. There comes a point that it's enough. The key is to decide what that point is before you need to know, because then you can build a win-win structure.

DAVID'S WISDOM
WIN-WIN

David was a key influence in moving me toward the true win-win. He had a way of structuring deals so fairly that if we were in negotiations with someone, I was more comfortable not being in the room and just taking what David emerged to say my share was. He taught me this in so many ways that I can't narrow it down to just one story.

It started with his own compensation. David was in the equities business. He invested in small companies. He took companies public. He took public companies and helped them expand. Any time he worked as a consultant, he refused to be reimbursed for expenses, and he also refused to be paid a fee up front. Instead, he took his compensation in the form of stock warrants. If the company's stock was valued at $2 a share at the time he signed on, he'd negotiate an option enabling him to buy a certain number of shares at $2.50. If he helped drive the price to $3 or $5 a share by a certain time, he'd exercise his warrant. He was willing to eat his own cooking.

When David was working with a public company on a restructuring deal because things weren't going so well, he would always speak up for the previous investors, for the shareholders who weren't in the room. Usually in that situation, no one cares about the previous money. Those guys lost their money, the thinking goes, and that's not my fault if I'm putting new money in. David saw it differently. "These are like the children in a divorce," he'd say. "If things are going bad, there's got to be somebody who stands up for the children."

David was that person.

CHASING THE SCREAM

I bought the documentary rights to a *New York Times* best-selling book about the war on drugs by Johann Hari called *Chasing the Scream*. It's an important topic to me personally, and I wanted this project out there more than I wanted to make money on it. Making a difference by telling the story was my highest operating value.

I brought in an Academy Award–winning producer. Together, we brought in an award-winning director and developed the book into a series. One after the other, HBO, Netflix, and the networks turned it down: it was too controversial, they already had something like it, and a series of other reasons. We ended up without many more places to pitch it.

We took it to a new company called Quibi, which did only short content, four to ten minutes long, optimized to be viewed on your phone. Steven Spielberg produced a series for them; lots of people did. They fell in love with our project and agreed to commission eight episodes. We were relieved—but we got millions less than we could have with a traditionally formatted documentary. There was a lot less money to work with.

My producing partners came back with a deal that made sense to them, where they would be paid to produce the episodes, but I would lose the majority of my investment, with some hope of recouping the money later by reusing the content. It was a win-lose deal and very easy to reject. "Hey," they said, "we don't have anywhere else to go with this. You're going to blow this deal." I explained to them that was fine. I wasn't doing a win-lose deal.

We went around again, and they suggested something that would mitigate my loss, but one of the producing partners would lose. "You don't understand," I said. "When I say I'm committed to a win-win deal, that means you have to win too." We went back to the table, and people had to adjust until we finally structured it into a win-win deal.

Unfortunately, one thing they suggested was that the author needed to take less. They wanted me to suggest a figure that wasn't fair, and when I came back with my own number, they thought it was too high.

I called Johann and said, "Look, we're all having to adjust because it's much smaller."

"What do you think I should get on it?" he said. And I told him my number, because it was what I thought he deserved.

"Yeah, that's fair," he said.

"Anything less doesn't feel right," I told him.

I went back to my partners, and we all had to contribute some money to make that number happen. But we did. I knew there'd be benefits beyond the impact of the film, too, in the form of credibility I could leverage on other projects.

We were in a place where we could have been a bully and forced a deal on Johann. It's just not the way it was going to happen. He wasn't part of the negotiations—and someone had to speak up for the "children," the parties who are affected but not in the room. That's the win-win-win—the deal that benefits all involved.

The series was delivered as I wrote this book. In the meantime, Quibi's investors shut the company down after it spent $1.2 billion of its $1.6 billion in funding. (See? I told you failure is always an option.) *Chasing the Scream* was one of the few series that Quibi actually decided to complete. (One more note: The deal we struck with Quibi is another example of playing a longer game. Two years from now, the rights to the footage revert to us, enabling us to repurpose the film for profit.)

Johann went on to write a second book called *Lost Connections* about depression. It's a beautiful, important book, another *New York Times* bestseller. I called Johann when I read an early draft and said I would love to license it for a film. Then he got a call from Oprah Winfrey, who had the book on her bedside table—and she wanted the rights. But one thing led to another, as can be the case with film projects, and in time Oprah gave him the rights back because she wasn't able to do the project.

I got a call from Johann. "Because of the way you treated me during the last deal, I want you to have the rights," he told me.

That's the power of building a win-win reputation. It's also a step toward building what I call real wealth, which we'll take up next. And it has nothing to do with money.

6

REAL WEALTH

To have a friend, you have to be a friend.

(FROM DAVID NEMELKA)

Back in our siding sales days, Red McMillan and I once knocked on the door of a man named Bill. I was young, so he looked old to me—maybe forty-five!—and he lived in a run-down little frame house, no more than 1,200 square feet. He had a Cadillac parked out front.

We pitched Bill on siding for his house, a $6,000 job. Aside from the Cadillac, you wouldn't have thought he had any money. But he bought the siding—cash deal.

Later, when we came by to check in with the installation crew, we found Bill out back in the swimming pool he'd just put in. We came to like him, and we'd talk while he was floating in his pool. It turned out Bill worked for the Santa Fe Railway, and he'd fallen off a boxcar at work and injured his back. He settled his claim for more than $100,000.

The only one among us who didn't realize Bill was on his way to being broke again was, well, Bill.

I tell this story to make a point about the difference between money and wealth. Money comes and goes, as Bill soon found out. Wealth is enduring. You can have money without ever becoming wealthy. Think of the lottery winners who spend their windfall as if they were allergic to it, then find themselves worse off than they were before they hit the jackpot.

I'm not talking about the soft aspects of wealth, either, like having your health and a good family, essential as they are. I'm speaking in the business sense. You can go from having a lot of money to being broke, and I've done it, but it's very hard to go from wealthy to broke. You could even say that real wealth is what you have left when you lose all your money.

RELATIONSHIPS, SKILLS, AND ASSETS

Real wealth is what you have left when you lose all your money. And by that I mean your skills and relationships.

As I write this, we're in the midst of a global pandemic. We've lived through crises before—9/11, the 2008 crash—but nobody walking the face of this earth has experienced what we're going through now. At one point, more than a trillion dollars in value disappeared from the stock market in a week's time. We're talking massive upheaval.

My partner, Patrick, and I saw an opportunity in the chaos and quickly planned a docuseries called *Crisis Investing 2020*. We approached twenty of the most brilliant crisis investment advisors to ask if they'd participate. Every one of them said yes—and it was all because of the relationships we had built over the years.

That's real wealth. It's the difference between moving through the world alone or in good company. I believe you could parachute me anywhere in the country with $10 in my pocket and, building off the relationships I've developed, I could find my way to success.

The first step to building leverageable business relationships is developing skills that make you valuable to others. I think of skills as the second aspect of real wealth, and from the relationships and skills comes a third, as a natural consequence: the assets that help you seize opportunities. It's a circular, self-feeding dynamic that fosters success.

MASTERMINDS

I've found no better way to build relationships than mastermind events. I've written earlier about them (especially in Chapter 3) and how much I spend—$170,000 a year or so—to participate. One of the best known is the Genius Network run by Joe Polish. Members pay $25,000 a year to attend an annual event that attracts hundreds as well as two or three of the monthly, small-group sessions that Joe holds at his office in Phoenix. There, forty to sixty of us will sit in a semicircle, each of us tasked with sharing an idea in a ten-minute talk that will deliver $250,000 in value to the others—that is, an idea you can bring into your business that returns $250,000. It's a process that forges relationships while fostering skills as well.

I'm a member of a couple of health masterminds. One has about five hundred people in it, at least half of them medical doctors or PhDs. The other, the Consumer Health Summit, brings the top thinkers in health care together once a year. When my film company needed to gather medical advice for a docuseries on cancer, we had a long list of contacts to call on. I have a friend who's a medical doctor, and his wife is a PhD. Sadly, their son contracted a rare cancer. They invited me to dinner to discuss his treatment options. I'm a high-school-dropout filmmaker, and I was exposing them to options they weren't aware of because of the relationships, skills, and assets I've developed through my work.

Another mastermind called the War Room included about 150 people who were all internet marketers. We gathered four times a year for two or three days at a time and covered a full curriculum on internet marketing. What was working? What wasn't working? I came back with notebooks full of information that I used to sharpen my saw. I'm a member of an entrepreneur mastermind that meets three times a year too. There's no better place for me to learn and recharge my batteries than in the company of entrepreneurs like me.

BEING OF VALUE

Because of the relationships they build and the skills they foster, masterminds are well worth what are significant investments of my time and money. But I actually measure the value of those investments not by what I get out of the events, but what I put in.

The key to building a relationship is to show up not for what you can get out of it, but with what you can put into it. At mastermind events, I can tell who's new. You can spot them as they work the room, almost as if they've brought a checklist of people they want to meet who will be of help to them. They won't find a foothold in the group. Everyone in the room can see their hidden agenda, and no one in the room is there to be treated as a prospect. Remember the story of the goose that laid the golden egg? These are new people who see the egg, but not the goose.

The people to whom I'm drawn show up looking to be of service. If you bring that spirit of "How can I be of service to you, what can I do for you?" into your relationships, you don't need to worry about collecting the other side. It will take care of itself.

SKILLS TO OFFER

To be of service and build relationships, you need not just a willingness to help but skills to offer. I used to be a business associate of Dr. Laura Schlessinger, the radio host who had twenty million listeners at the top of her game. A psychologist and dear friend in Salt Lake wanted a radio show of her own, and she asked for an introduction. I was happy to do it, but only once, and so I asked my friend: Are you sure the time is now?

A relationship with Dr. Laura could catapult her to success, but only if she were ready for success. She had no demo tapes to share, no radio show in the local market, no skills, and no evidence of early success. She started a local show, and sure enough people called in to share their problems and seek her help. After a couple years, my friend succeeded in developing the skills that could leverage a relationship.

Jimmy Iovine is an entrepreneur and recording executive who founded Beats Electronics with Dr. Dre. After building the company together, they sold it to Apple for $3 billion. I've heard him attribute his success to always asking the question, "How can I be of service?" When he started, he was an intern, the guy who swept the recording studio in exchange for an opportunity to apprentice in engineering. One day on a holiday, no one wanted to work. He got a call asking him to come engineer a session. They didn't tell him who it was; it was just a low-paying engineering session. He said yes. The musician was John Lennon, and out of that session grew a relationship that propelled Iovine into his career. With time and success, Jimmy became the subject of one of the most inspiring entrepreneurial docuseries I've ever seen, following him from the very beginning all the way to becoming a billionaire. He has always attributed his success to the "How can I be of service?" mentality. But you shouldn't overlook the fact that he's a spectacularly talented veteran of the music industry who invested the time to develop his skills.

HERE FOR YOU

Mike Myers, the *Saturday Night Live* alumni turned film star—for example, playing the character Austin Powers—made his documentary director's debut with a 2013 film titled *Supermensch* about the legendary talent manager Shep

Gordon. The title of the film embarrassed Shep, but in the end he embraced it and used the same title on the book he later wrote about his philosophy and career.

A few years later, when I sat down for lunch at a master-mind event, a guy I recognized approached, gestured to the empty seat at my side, and asked if he could sit there. It was Shep Gordon, one of my heroes and a surprise guest at the event. He's the paragon of building relationships based on service. I spent the next hour drilling Shep with questions and soaking up everything he had to say.

The list of superstars Shep has represented include Alice Cooper, Blondie, Teddy Pendergrass, Sammy Hagar, and Pink Floyd—and he's never had a written agreement with anybody. Shep operates by the philosophy that if he can't trust his clients, they shouldn't be clients. They reciprocate. When Hagar founded Cabo Wabo Tequila and the restaurant and nightclub chain of the same name, he brought Shep into the deal on nothing but a handshake.

Shep told me that when other talent managers pick his brain, they spend their time with him asking how they can do better. How do they become more effective? How can they make more money? Not once, he told me, had one of them asked him how they could make their clients more money: How do I be a better manager for my client?

That's the question Shep wakes up every morning asking himself. How can he make more money for Alice Cooper so his client has a better and easier life? That's Shep's entire focus—and it's the question no one else bothers to ask him, or themselves. His success is no accident.

DAVID'S WISDOM
ONE IN A MILLION

David's wife, Ingrid, was the love of his life, the greatest of his many relationships. He always did something fun to mark her birthday, and one year as the date approached, he asked her, "Where would you like to go to lunch on your birthday?"

As she was thinking it over, he said, "How about that place where you and the women from church like to go?"

He was talking about the Golden Corral. I'm not going to say much about his culinary choices, but in Mapleton, Utah, where they lived, there's not a big selection.

The next day, David took Ingrid to the Golden Corral. As soon as they walked in, balloons dropped from the ceiling, a TV crew popped out, and the manager rushed over with a big certificate. It was a huge celebration. Ingrid was Golden Corral's one-millionth customer . . . and she had won a brand-new car! The dealer walked her outside, showed her the car, and Ingrid relished her birthday lunch.

It was the amazing coincidental event of a lifetime. After lunch Ingrid drove happily around town, visiting the kids and grandkids, showing the car and telling the story.

When they got home, David dropped to his knee as if he were ready to propose all over again. Instead of a ring, he gave her a card.

There was no one-millionth customer. Those were not news cameras; that was a crew he hired. He'd bought her the car a few days before.

"This is for you, Ingrid," the card said, "because you're one in a million."

That's wealth, given and received, as only David could do it.

SHOWING HUMILITY

I have a friend, David Lewine, who's a brilliant, forward-thinking guy. He got his master's in journalism and in business at Columbia University, he was president of Jane Fonda's fitness company, and he was one of the founders of Playboy Home Video. I noticed that any time David started a project, he would make appointments with people, including me, so he could ask them questions. "Hey," he'd say, "I'm thinking about doing this. What do you think?" Usually entrepreneurs who do that are so in love with their own idea that they can't tolerate any criticism. You can feel the defensiveness kick in.

David was the opposite. He would take careful notes and consider everything he heard. "I hadn't thought about that," he'd say. "Boy, I'm glad you said that. Really good point." I'm sure some of what he heard was helpful to him—but the experience was always gratifying for me, to be approached by a very bright man who genuinely wanted your help in thinking something through. I always felt closer to him afterward.

Over time David developed deep relationships with a multitude of powerful people, in part because of his humility and his willingness to ask for advice. It turns out that there was a psychological principle at work in his approach, because we tend to think highly of people who ask us for advice. I don't believe David was doing this to manipulate. It was a side effect of his thoughtful, humble personality. But by allowing others to help him, he strengthened the relationships he enjoyed with all of his friends.

GROWING BY GIVING

I have a mentor named Louis Sportelli who built a successful chiropractic practice in a very small town in Pennsylvania. He ended up serving as chairman of the American Chiropractic Association as well as the primary malpractice insurance company for chiropractors. Without a doubt, he was the single most powerful voice in the chiropractic profession.

Soon after I met him, I got a thank-you note in the mail, and then a month later a book with a sticker in it: "From the library of Louis Sportelli," signed to Jeff Hays. He'd sent a letter along with it saying why he thought it might be interesting to me. Over the next several years, I averaged a book from Louis every two to three months with a handwritten note: "Hey, thinking of you. This book reminded me of you, thought you would like it."

I'm well known for never wearing a tie, but one year on my birthday, a package arrived with a Brioni tie inside, a very expensive Italian designer brand. Louis had pulled it out of the box and tied it, then put it back in the box with a note: "Jeff, I took this out and tied it because I know you don't know how to tie one of these things."

He doesn't do this only with me. He does it with everyone. Every high school student who graduated in his town in Pennsylvania got a book from Louis called *1,001 Careers* with a note made out to the graduate, saying, "Congratulations on graduating from high school. It proves you can finish something. You notice in the book I underlined 'chiropractic.' I don't want to steer you in one direction or another, but if you're ever interested in that career, call me and I'd be happy to tell you my experience. I wanted to send you this just to congratulate you for your accomplishment." He did this for decades.

Every day, Louis buys five $1 lottery tickets. When the guy at the car wash does a great job, when somebody smiles at the grocery store, he captures their name and sends them a note with a lottery ticket: "Hey, thank you for doing such a great job on my car. I hope you win a million bucks." Can you imagine the effect? This is how you build a multimillion-dollar practice in a small town—one relationship at a time. The income he earns, that's money. But the relationships? That's wealth.

BUILDING A REPUTATION

Part of building relationships is building a reputation, and that's tricky. You're in control of your behavior and what you produce, but you can't really control other people's perceptions. I know plenty of marvelous people who've been maligned. At some point in their career, everybody is going to have competitors who intentionally try to bring them down or others who unintentionally misunderstand them.

I've learned to think of my reputation as more than something I have. It's something I manage. The simplest way to do it is to insist on the true win-win deals we covered in Chapter 5. When things go wrong—as they sometimes will, despite your best intentions—and you make a mess, clean it up. My formula is to make amends where I can and make peace where I can't. There is no shame in failure or mistakes. I've actually come to believe that shame is totally useless. It's not even penance.

At mastermind events, people tend to introduce me by exaggerating my accomplishments. I've seen others also introduced this way. A couple of people do it so often that it's clear they're exaggerating the achievements of everybody they associate with to make themselves look better. So, when I hear someone introduce me like this onstage—"Here's Jeff Hays, the Academy Award–winning documentarian"—I feel my face go ashen. The first thing I'll do is thank them for the compliment and set the record straight: I was short-listed for an Academy Award, but I was neither nominated for one nor awarded one. Preventing other people from stretching your reputation is as important to maintaining it as anything else you do.

STARTING IN THE RIGHT GEAR

I've learned that I can't start a car in fourth gear. If you've ever driven a stick shift, you know what I mean. You start

your car, miss first gear, accidentally land in third instead—
and the car stalls. You need to be in first gear to get moving.

It doesn't mean the car's broken. It doesn't mean that the
transmission's failed or that the engine's died. You're just in
the wrong gear.

Skills and relationships work the same way. With experience I've learned to begin with a clear-eyed assessment:
What are my real skills, and what are the relationships I can
call on? Based on where you want to go, more questions
follow: What are the skills and relationships that I need to
get there? And you invest in developing them.

There's never been a better time to develop skills.
Whatever it is that you want to accomplish, someone has
written a book on it. Lots of people have probably written
crappy books on it, so you have to sort through the noise to
find the real stuff. But it's there. You can learn everything
from cooking a perfect egg to folding a long cord to writing
software on YouTube videos.

Still, I've learned to be realistic about this. Developing
the skills you need to succeed will take time. Remember the
ten-thousand-hour rule that Malcolm Gladwell wrote about
for achieving mastery of a particular skill? It was a linchpin
of his book *Outliers: The Story of Success.* Gladwell's rule has
since been challenged by researchers, but the basic point he
makes holds: developing skills takes time. The good news in
this is that, when you invest the time, you can develop the
skills. I took two years of Spanish in school, but I can't speak
Spanish. That left me believing that some people can learn
a new language and others—including me—simply can't.
But it turns out that anyone can learn a language if they put

in the time. To become moderately proficient in Spanish takes about eight hundred hours of study. Why didn't I learn Spanish in junior high? Because at forty-five minutes a day, the math doesn't add up. If you were to devote two hours a day to studying Spanish, five days a week, you'd need eighty weeks to do it. The time required varies with the language. Russian? You can learn it—if you're willing to spend 1,600 hours in study.

As I became known, people began inviting me to lunch to pick my brain about everything from making a documentary to building an email list for crowdfunding. They seemed to think that if they spent forty-five minutes with me over a cup of coffee, they'd leave with the skills they needed to do any or all of the above. They were totally sincere in this belief, and off they'd go. They thought with one conversation they had it all—when, in fact, all I'd really been able to show them in forty-five minutes was the tip of the iceberg. I'd spent a lifetime developing these skills. Time after time, their projects would fail and they wouldn't know why. It's for the same reason that you wouldn't invite a doctor to dinner and say, "Hey, listen, I'd like to pick your brain about the appendix. I'm thinking about taking mine out. Can you walk me through the steps?"

There are no shortcuts to developing skills. As important as what you know is understanding what you don't yet know—which is to say, recognizing what gear you're in. Otherwise, you're just going to jump in your car with someplace to go and stall before you even get going.

READY TO ROLL?

I hope I've convinced you of the importance of developing relationships through service based on skills. It's the essence of wealth and, for me at least, the key to success in life and business. I wouldn't want to send you into a mastermind event without skills you can bring to the table. So, next, let's talk about skills—the tools I've learned to keep in my toolbox and how to use them.

PART TWO

TOOLS

7

MARKETING

Don't fall in love with your product.
Fall in love with your customer.

(FROM JAY ABRAHAM)

I can identify the seminal pivot point in the development of my documentary film business. It was at a mastermind event I attended in 2013. I was in a room of two hundred people, wondering if I would regret the $25,000 I had spent to be there. Sitting at my table was a guy named Paul Hoffman. We introduced ourselves and struck up a conversation about our ventures.

"Do you have an email list?" Paul asked.

An email list? "Well, yeah," I said, "but it's small." About eight thousand addresses.

"How does someone get on it?" he asked.

"They buy something."

"You don't collect email addresses from anyone other than buyers?" Paul said.

At about this point, sitting there in the midst of this Genius event, I realized that I was a complete idiot. If you went to the website for my film company or any other business I had a hand in, there wasn't even a spot where you could enter your email address if you wanted to. Once you bought something and landed on my list, I did virtually nothing with it.

In large part, marketing is about channels, and email is a vital one. As soon as I got home, I fixed the website. If you wanted to watch one of my films, I didn't ask for money; I asked for your email address. I now have an active list of more than a million, and I can count on it to produce hundreds of thousands of dollars in a month—up from zero in 2013. And that all began when I sat at a table with Paul Hoffman. Even better, Paul is now one of my best friends.

SALES AND MARKETING

People sometimes confuse sales and marketing, or think of them as the same thing. They're not. They're two separate arenas, two separate skills. Understanding the importance of marketing begins with recognizing that distinction.

The difference between the two became very clear to me when I made the film *Fahrenhype 9/11*. Prior to that, I'd made children's films at Capstone Entertainment that we sold over the phone. We had to sell every copy. No one called Capstone Entertainment to ask, "Hey, have you guys got any children's films we could buy?" It was on us, proactively, to go out and prospect and pitch and close every last copy. That's sales.

With *Fahrenhype 9/11*, there was such a vacuum in the market, such an opening for a film making the counter-argument to Michael Moore's blockbuster *Fahrenheit 9/11*, that we just had to make the film. Walmart agreed to buy a hundred thousand copies. We put it on the shelf at Blockbuster, and people walked up to buy it. We simply had to let people know it existed by running ads, and then place it in stores. That's marketing.

The job of marketing is to build a brand, generate leads, and create familiarity with your product so that when a salesperson goes to sell it, their job is easier. The very best marketing does more than that. It makes sales automatic.

Don't conflate the two. You need a marketing manager to run your marketing and a sales manager to run your sales.

NO ONE BUT YOU

I suppose one point of my opening story about Paul Hoffman and my email list goes back to Chapter 6 on true wealth, which is rooted in your relationships. Here's another: if you're an entrepreneur, no matter what your business, you're going to have to master the skills of marketing. You can't outsource it, no matter how much you want to. If you don't do it, someone like me is going to come along and eat your lunch. It's just a fact.

I belong to a mastermind group called Mindshare run by JJ Virgin, the bestselling author, fitness guru, and entrepreneur. It's a sizable group of about six hundred, often physicians or others in the health and wellness space, and it's focused on health marketing. It has more *New York Times* bestselling authors than any other group of which I'm part. It's terrific for people who are making the transition out of fee-based, time-for-money work to a different model offering more freedom and greater reach. JJ's mastermind teaches the marketing skills needed to succeed: self-promotion through writing a book, building a website, developing a line of products.

I'd hear the same thing over and over at Mindshare events: "Who can I find to do this for me?" Most of the people in the group have money, and they're looking to buy their way out of learning the marketing skills themselves. They'll happily pay someone $150,000 or $200,000 a year to manage their marketing—and they're doomed to failure.

What they're really saying is, "Hey, I'll pay you $200,000 a year to make me $2 million."

Once people discover they can really make you $2 million with their marketing skills, they're not going to make you the $2 million anymore. They're going to make it for themselves. It's common for top copywriters who've built a reputation to earn more than $1 million a year writing direct mail pieces and website offers. They're in business for themselves, not you.

Even if you manage to find one of these folks on the way up, they're a ticking time bomb. Once they realize the value of their skills, they're sure to leave.

If you're going to own a business, you're going to have to invest the time required to learn how to market. It's the single most valuable skill you can develop, because it's the multiplier of everything else you have. David Nemelka used to tell me that your idea is 20 percent of success; the other 80 percent is marketing. Even when you build the momentum that carries your business to the second level, and you can afford a marketing team, it's still on you to conceive and oversee the execution of your marketing plan—and it will be until you've built a very successful company.

Don't outsource your marketing. I've found that most marketing agencies are spectacular at marketing one thing, and that's their agency. It's astounding. They're best not at marketing for you, but to you.

This is a hill you have to climb. In this chapter, I want to share some tools that will help you along the way. It's a distillation of a lifetime's worth of marketing experience and training. You could write a book on each of these topics. Think of this chapter as the CliffsNotes study guide, pointing you toward where you should focus your studies.

LEVELING UP

Your goal, always, should be what I call third-level marketing.

First-level marketing is the trap that snares companies that aren't smart or mature enough to avoid the trap. You can spot first-level marketing by the ads and other communications that always lead with the features of your product: "Check out our new gizmo glass screen protector for your iPhone!"

Second-level marketers are smarter. "It's not the features," they say. "It's the benefits." "Put our new screen protector on your iPhone to prevent scratches and breaks!" The formula for rising to this level begins with the phrase "so that." As soon as you write down the feature in your product, you follow with the phrase: "Put our new gizmo screen protector on your iPhone *so that* you don't get scratches and breaks." All it takes to connect features to benefits are these two simple words.

Third-level marketing is king of the hill. It's not about features; it's not about benefits. It's about who I become when I buy your product. It carries you to an emotion. "Check out the cool kids at the party—all rocking their gizmo glass!"

Let me give you a real example: the GoPro camera. My friend Ron Lynch, one of the most brilliant marketers I know, crafted the advertising. He could have talked about how rugged the camera is, how it's waterproof, small, light. That's first-level marketing. He could have talked about how you can take it everywhere you go—mountain biking, skydiving, wherever and whatever. That's second level. But there are lots of cameras out there with similar features and benefits.

Instead, GoPro got customers to submit the videos they took as they did extraordinary things. Flying off mountaintops in body suits, performing balancing acts on mountain bikes along a razor-edge ridge, dangling from a sheer cliff face by the strength of one hand. Ron's message: If you buy a GoPro, you're an adventurer, a hero. That's third-level marketing at its best.

KIDS DON'T DRIVE

It's a Disney phrase: kids don't drive. They realized long ago that you can't just market a kids' film to kids because they can't get to the movies by themselves. If you're selling a kids' film, you've got to sell Mom and Dad on the movie too. Disney wasn't alone in acting on this insight. If you look at the Warner Brothers cartoons from the forties, fifties, and early sixties, you'll see they're filled with double entendres that kids have no chance of getting. They're there because they leave Mom and Dad laughing. DreamWorks still uses the formula.

The lesson is that, in marketing, you've got to be aware of everyone involved in the decision to buy. If you're selling a product to women, you've got to give them the ammunition to explain to their spouses why this is a smart, logical choice. If you're marketing to men, the same thing applies.

You're never just marketing to your prospects. You're marketing to their friends, who will judge their decision, and their significant other, who'll want to know why they did it.

MISTAKING YOURSELF FOR THE HERO

We've all seen the ads. Maybe it's a furniture store: "My great-grandfather started this store; we've been here in the county since 1924; we're members of the Better Business Bureau and the Chamber." It's all about them, them, and them. This is first-level marketing at its most abused.

The audience looking at their ad does not care about anyone's great-grandfather. They want to know: Do they have great furniture at great prices with great delivery, great service, and great follow-up? And at the second level: "How comfortable will my grandfather be when he sits on my new recliner?" At the third level: "What are my neighbors going to think of my new living room? Will I get invited to the better cocktail parties?"

Don't make the mistake of thinking that you're the product. Don't make yourself the hero of your own story, the Luke Skywalker. The audience, your customers, they're Luke. You're their Yoda. I actually use this as a rule of thumb when I'm starting a project: Make them Luke, make me Yoda. Mmm, my young Skyshopper. The Force is strong with you. Guide you I will!

KEEPING IT SIMPLE

As I've worked with our copywriters in recent years, I'll ask them a question: "What would Trump say?" It's not intended as a political comment. It's a marketing comment. For years, the rule of thumb for marketers was to aim their copy at a fifth- to seventh-grade level—and preferably the fifth. It was the accepted norm.

Then I watched Donald Trump, along with the rest of us. He speaks at what might be a second- or third-grade level—again, no judgment, just observation—and never has a president communicated more effectively with his base. People forget: a 100 IQ is average, which means that 50 percent of the people you're communicating with have a two-digit IQ, no matter whether you're marketing a political campaign, a film, or a widget.

To make ourselves sound smart, we often try to speak as if we're smart. Real communicators know that if they're trying to reach a mass audience, even fifth grade to seventh grade may be far too advanced.

The simpler you speak, the more repeatable your concepts, the better off you'll be.

THE IRRESISTIBLE OFFER

The key to all your offers is to make them irresistible. You can do this by removing any sense of risk for the customer. After all, even with a free offer, there's risk. You're asking customers to invest their time and share their email address. Will it be worth it?

We might answer that question by adding bonuses. Think back to the old direct response ads on TV, the ones that keep asking, "Now how much would you pay?" If they're selling gloves, they keep stacking on value, adding a cap, a scarf, whatever it takes until the offer is irresistible.

But we've often found the best way to make an offer irresistible is to make it scarce. You've heard this before: "Be one of the first hundred people to call our 800 number, before they're all gone! You need to act *now*!"

There's a marketing guru in Florida named Dean Jackson who likes to talk about his Mafia offer—the one you can't refuse. He's a master. He once sent me a piece offering a $5,000 marketing seminar. I thought about going, but just couldn't decide. What if I spent the $5,000 and didn't come back with any ideas that turn into money? I didn't commit. The next email I got said, "Fly yourself down here for the seminar, and you can pay me thirty days after—and then only if you feel like you got $5,000 in value." That's a Mafia offer. I didn't refuse.

THE CORE CATALYZING STATEMENT

The core catalyzing statement encapsulates the purpose of your business, the essential selling proposition that you take to the marketplace. The shorter and simpler, the better. Your marketing flows from it.

One of the best of all time comes from FedEx: "When it absolutely, positively has to be there overnight." They haven't used it for some time, but it laid the foundational understanding—It needs to be there tomorrow? Let's FedEx it—upon which they've built their entire business. Another great example comes from Domino's Pizza: *Pizza in thirty minutes or it's free.* If you're looking for the world's greatest pizza, you're not going to think of Domino's. But if you need it there fast because the kids are hungry and you haven't planned dinner, then it's Domino's to the rescue. For Jeff Hays Films, our core catalyzing statement is: *Movies that make movements.* It may be even more important to us internally than it is externally. When we don't keep it front and center in our own thinking, we get a film like our dive into the world of wine—a movie without a movement—and we regret it.

THE UNIQUE SELLING PROPOSITION

The concept of the unique selling proposition, or USP, was promoted by Jay Abraham, a marketing guru, about twenty-five years ago. It starts with a question: What is it about you that sets you apart from your competitors? What's the one reason a customer with choices would come to you? If you're in the furniture business in Salt Lake City, your

USP might be that you're the only furniture store in the city that has a direct relationship with Scandinavian furniture makers—no middleman, a bigger selection than anyone else, all because of that connection. Now you're not just one more furniture store; you're something special.

Jay's concept was revolutionary for its time, but most everyone is doing it now. If you're not, you're playing at a disadvantage. You've got to spend time focused on your business and what makes you unique, and offer that to your market.

The next level in this thinking is the unique selling mechanism, or USM, a concept used by Agora Publishing, a brilliant marketer. The USP is about you. The USM takes the same concept and makes it about your customers. What is it about your product that will make customers succeed when they've failed so many times in the past? It's beautifully suited to the supplement business. Let's say your USP is that you offer the purest fish oil on the market. The USM? What makes it work when others don't is the particle size, just a tenth of the normal size, so your body can absorb it as intended.

Just to be clear: I'm making this up by way of example. I'm not selling fish oil.

DAVID'S WISDOM
TODAY IS KIDS' DAY

David's birthday was on March 26. But he didn't make it about himself. He made it all about his twenty-eight grandkids. Kids' Day, he called it.

Every Kids' Day, David rented a bus and took the whole day off. No parents allowed. He and the grand-kids would make a list of all the things they wanted to do. They wanted to go swimming. They wanted to ride horses. They wanted to get ice cream. They wanted to go to the movies. And every last thing they wanted, they did.

David would take that whole tribe to a theater and watch ten minutes of a movie. Then they'd go get ice cream. All packed in, all day long. Because David wasn't the hero of his own birthday story; the grandkids were.

David had seven kids, and as he was raising them, he had a hobby or a sport or an activity that he would do with each of his children. Not with any of the others, just with the one child who chose it. He and one son raised world champion racing pigeons. With another child, he raised Appaloosa horses. With a third, miniature horses and another world champion. And with another one, quarter horse racing. He had a lot of kids, and a lot on his plate. But this was his way of making sure that each of them knew they were special—and special to him.

THREE WAYS TO GROW

At the risk of dropping another triad on you, here we go. It comes from Jay Abraham: there are only three ways to grow your business.

- The first is to increase your number of customers. This is the most obvious choice, and it's where most people camp out. It's also the hardest and most expensive part of building your business. These next two are easier, and they're too often overlooked.

- The second is to increase the amount your customers buy. Would you like to supersize your order?
- The third is to increase how often your customers buy. Sign up for a monthly refill and you'll get a discount!

Chiropractors were famous for camping on the first option, on acquiring customers. As I worked on my film about their industry, I'd ask about their biggest need, and almost all would answer with a stream of new patients. And that's what they'd do, mailing out flyers, buying big ads in the newspapers, offering free spinal exams in the mall. It's laborious work, especially when customers are going out your back door as fast or faster than you're bringing them in through the front door.

But then, about thirty years ago, some smart marketing gurus began pointing them toward the easier options. Once you get someone in the door, the gurus said, you've got somebody who's inclined to believe what you tell them. That led to their own version of the second option, supersizing: nutritional training, nutritional supplements, more products their existing customers could buy to improve their health. And that led to their version of the third option, frequency. Instead of simply waiting for their patients to get another crick in their neck and return for another treatment, chiropractors began offering wellness plans. Pay a monthly fee and come as often as you want. Put your family on a plan and come on a monthly basis.

I met chiropractors whose businesses were starving to death, because they didn't embrace these options. And I saw chiropractors who were making a million dollars a year because they did.

It's not new wisdom. Back in the early 1900s, when Rexall was selling milkshakes in its drugstores, the great marketing guru Elmer Wheeler gave Rexall a new pitch. Whenever someone ordered a shake, he'd have the druggist hold up one egg in one hand and two eggs in the other. "One egg or two?" A lot of people who didn't want an egg would say one. A lot of people who wanted one egg would say two. And Rexall sold millions more eggs.

Chiropractors are not the only ones to apply this wisdom; far from it. It's difficult to remember, but there was a time when Apple was in such bad shape that Microsoft had to invest a hundred million dollars in its rival to keep it from going out of business. That's because Microsoft feared that, as the last one standing, it would face legal attacks as a monopoly. Today Apple has grown so much that it's the bigger company, with a market capitalization that exceeds the rival that rescued it.

What catapulted Apple into the stratosphere was the iPod. Once Apple got people using the iPod with that Steve Jobs line, "a thousand songs in your pocket," it slowly started leading customers to a Mac computer and the suite of products that followed, from the MacBook to the iPad and, as I write this, the iPhone 14. Once you owned one Apple product, it became easier to buy the others, because they all worked so beautifully together.

Incidentally, I spent a million dollars in a legal fight with Apple over the name of what was then my business, Podfitness—and I still bought every product that Apple produced, all building off the entry-point product that got me started. No one's better than Apple at leading customers down the road of deeper and deeper commitment, with bigger purchases and greater frequency.

FUNNEL POWER

Jeff Walker is a marketer who wrote a *New York Times* best-seller titled *Launch*. The subtitle really tells the story: *An Internet Millionaire's Secret Formula to Sell Almost Anything Online, Build a Business You Love, and Live the Life of Your Dreams.* He launched the book by giving it away; anyone who paid $7.95 for shipping and handling got a copy for free. His cost on each book was $21, and he was only taking in $7.95. He lost significant money on each book that went out the door. And it worked—he shipped a lot of books.

For Jeff, that transaction was simply the first step in a funnel. On the order page, he added what's called an "order bump." An upsell, something else they could buy. And after the transaction closed, he offered something more—what's called a "one-click upsell."

The big-ticket item was a how-to course that Jeff normally sold for $2,000. He dropped the price on it to $200 and put it in his funnel. It tanked. Then he looked again at his pitch: "This is normally $2,000 and you can get it for $200!" First-level, second-level marketing. He took it to the third level: "If you take this course, this is how your life will be transformed! And by the way, it's normally $2,000 but you can have it for $200."

Sales soared. So many people bought the upsell that instead of losing $13 a book, he made $27 for every book he gave away. That allowed him to scale the campaign dramatically, and he drove so many sales through so many channels that his free-book giveaway carried him all the way to the bestseller list.

Lead Magnets and Trip Wires

We sometimes refer to the first offer in this approach as the "lead magnet": an offer that's all but impossible to refuse, leading to a logical series of subsequent offers that work together to increase the amount your customers buy.

Much as I hate to think of my customers as battlefield casualties, we'll sometimes place what we call a "trip wire" in their path. We take our main product and knock a smaller piece off of it. That's our trip wire, our lead magnet.

EXTENDING THE FUNNEL

Put all these ways to grow together—lead magnets, trip wires, a series of products—and you've got the makings of a powerful marketing program. It begins with bringing people in, and once they're there, leading them to buy more. Once you've got a product in the market, your challenge is lengthening the funnel: What would somebody who bought this want next?

For example, let's take square-foot gardening, the practice of dividing a small growing area into smaller sections, typically one square foot each. Your lead magnet? A free video on raising award-winning tomatoes in a square-foot garden. Your trip wire? Plans for assembling the customer's own square-foot garden using items from the local hardware store that cost less than $40. Next comes a paid video on feasting on fresh vegetables all summer and canned vegetables through the winter using a square-foot garden that'll fit in a four-by-four section of the customer's backyard or rooftop. What else might your customers need? Fertilizer made especially for their square-foot garden and seeds for their square-foot garden shipped directly to their door. A two-hour, step-by-step video on building and tending square-foot gardens. Last? How about sending two guys over to build a square-foot garden for the customer?

We'll do this with our docuseries. After the free run is over, we'll offer a replay weekend. Two weeks after that, a flash drive sale. Each one of these increases our average order value by 10 to 15 percent, and sometimes as much as 20 percent.

FIVE WAYS TO OPTIMIZE

In my business, we've expanded on Jay's list of three ways to grow a business, so we talk about five ways to optimize our marketing.

The first is optimizing our leads. Every business I've had has to have leads. As we've just covered, bringing more people in the front door is expensive—and it's critical to minimize those costs. You may be doing Facebook ads, Google AdWords, TV or radio ads. Whatever it is, we've learned to look at where our leads are coming from, what it's costing, and how many convert to profitable customers. You start to hone in on your best lead sources.

Starting in 2015, it was Facebook. That's no surprise. Facebook has spent billions of dollars optimizing its advertising services. When you upload your customer list into Facebook, they'll use the email addresses to find Facebook users. Then Facebook can look at your best customers and deliver your ads to mirror audiences who match their characteristics. Now you're leveraging the billions Facebook has invested to optimize your leads and drive your business.

Second, we optimize for conversion. This is about converting those leads into buyers. It translates into A/B split testing different messages and images on our website. We'll build multiple versions of our landing page and drive people to them with Facebook ads, then compare to see which converts better. You can optimize down to the color of a button and the words on the page. The work is never done. You continue to test and test and test, improving your conversion rate every step of the way.

You'll be surprised by what you learn through testing. I thought the best way to promote a docuseries was to put photos of all thirty people who were in it on the landing page. I was sure it would work. But we found that putting less information on the page drove more clicks. When we threw too much information at people, they'd get lost.

The third way is average order value—that's Jay's second way. When someone makes a purchase, we'll try an order bump: What would you like to add to this order? If you're buying a nutritional product, the bump might say, buy three more and we'll give you a fourth one free. Once they've made their purchase and entered their credit card, we don't bring them directly to our thank-you page. Instead they land on an upsell offer. It's the equivalent of standing at the checkout counter and noticing the mints. You've entered your credit card; one click and you can buy more!

The fourth way is also on Jay's list: How can we increase the frequency of customer buys? For some businesses, that means getting them in more often. It can mean sending an email a week after their purchase offering a different product, or more of the same one rather than waiting for them to run out.

And fifth, we look at margin. How can we spend less to make what we sell? Can I order in bulk? Order components and assemble them ourselves?

The effect of this approach can be powerful. If we can deliver just a 10 percent improvement in each of these areas, a 10 percent step toward optimization, we'll realize more than a 100 percent return overall because of the multiplier effect.

No one is better at optimization than Amazon, which started by selling just books. Its first step was getting customers to buy more books: "Hey, people who bought the same book as you also bought this book, and that one." I remember when Amazon started offering me something other than books. I thought it was the stupidest idea ever. Why would I buy an electric razor from Amazon? Well, a year later, I'm not only buying my electric razor from

Amazon, I'm buying my replacement heads, my cleaner, and on and on. Amazon optimized the buying experience; it optimized delivery. It optimized every aspect of its business for customer satisfaction, to the point that we've all simply watched Amazon slowly take over the world. I'm not saying that's good or bad. It just is.

And that's the power of optimization.

Sometimes as marketers, we'll get together and ask one another, "What are you optimizing for? Is it leads?" I might want more people coming down my funnel. Generally if we optimize for that, conversions will suffer. So, after optimizing for leads for a while, we might shift to conversion. A while later, maybe it's back-end sales. Facebook facilitates this.

And it's not just about business. You can optimize for sales—and you can also optimize for life. I once had a marketer ask me: "What are you optimizing in life right now?" It's a spectacular question. Maybe it's income, which means you're taking time away from family. Maybe it's your marriage or family. Maybe it's spirituality. What works in business—optimization—works in life.

BUILD YOUR AUDIENCE

In today's tech-driven world, your marketing options are always changing. I've found that the key to success is finding an audience that's yours to market to.

People build audiences of as many as five hundred thousand or seven hundred thousand followers on YouTube, Facebook, or Instagram, and you can definitely convert these followers into income. But if you survey businesses, you'll find that an old-fashioned approach—email—is still almost everyone's top marketing channel for generating revenue.

There's a lot wrong with email marketing, from deliverability issues to the noise in the marketplace, but it's still the most profitable component of most direct marketers' business. It's certainly the most profitable part of mine. And if you've got an email list, you may never go broke. You can literally shut your business down, and if all you're left with is a list of people who will open and read your emails, you've got something you can sell to someone else.

David Nemelka used to tell me, "Jeff, you've got to be planting crops that you're not going to harvest for a year, because they're the seeds of your future success." Investing in an email list is investing in that future.

Sprinkling Gold Dust

One of my important business coaches, Roger Hamilton, likes to talk about the challenge of building your list in terms of sprinkling gold dust: the things you can do to build your email list for free or at a very low cost. The possibilities are limited only by your imagination.

You can do quizzes. One of the most successful viral quizzes of all time was, "What Disney character are you?" You can do tests: "How high is your sleep IQ?" You can circulate petitions, you can give awards in your industry (the Top 10 Fitness Instructors in the United States). You can run contests. The key is to create a quiz or a test or a contest that relates to the problem your product can solve.

Sally Hogshead, a friend and author of bestsellers like *Fascinate* and *How the World Sees You*, has come up with an online quiz that gives those who take it real insight into their own personality. What's brilliant about it is that other marketers send it out to their lists because people like to take it—big marketers, with hundreds of thousands of names on their list.

Once they do, Sally shares the results of the quiz with the marketer, who comes away with a better understanding of how to talk to their customers. And in the process, Sally adds hundreds of thousands of new emails to *her* list, and at virtually no cost.

I've had success with petitions. As we prepared to release the film *GMOs Revealed*, we circulated a petition demanding full and accurate reporting on GMOs. At the bottom, we gave people who signed it the opportunity for a free viewing of *GMOs Revealed*. The effort yielded a list with seventy thousand emails. A few years ago, when the French government was considering treating vitamins and minerals as drugs, a nutraceutical manufacturer that made those products circulated a petition: Don't let the government of France take away your vitamin C and your supplements! They added a million names to their list in thirty days.

Petitioner beware: One key to success with your gold dust is making sure you, and not a third-party vendor, harvest the emails. When people think of online petitions, they think of the platform change.org. But if you use it, you won't get the emails; change.org will. We built our own petition platform using a WordPress site and a little bit of code, so the emails we gathered were ours.

Offering Value

The most direct way to build your list involves spending money, by offering something of value—an instructional video, an e-book, anything that offers a piece of information valuable enough for people who click on your paid Facebook ad to provide their email in exchange for receiving your offer. The offer can be of any size—as simple as explaining a new wrinkle in a diet—so long as it offers value to the recipient.

A friend of mine named Drew Manning went big in this direction, literally. Drew is a trainer with a company called Fit2Fat2Fit. He'd been athletic and fit his whole life, and he never understood how people got fat and why they had trouble working out. So, Drew stopped working out and went on the SAD diet—the Standard American Diet—for four long months. He gained seventy pounds! Then he lost the weight, so he knew what his clients were putting themselves through. He wrote about the experience, which led to a TV show on the A&E Network. Now he's doing it again, at forty years old. He's gained thirty pounds in thirty days, and he's tracking it on Facebook so followers can watch him put on the pounds. They'll have an opportunity to join him when it's time for the weight to come off. In the process of doing something fascinating, he's built a massive Facebook group and a massive email list that he can monetize by selling supplements and other products.

Step by Step, to 100,000

However you approach building your own list, getting an email isn't the end of your work; it's your beginning. When people enter their email, you're still at a transactional stage. Generally, we'll place them in a nurture campaign, continuing to send them new content in the arena that interests them. We're aiming to foster a two-way relationship from which we can build.

Consider setting your first target in growing your list at one hundred thousand recipients—big enough for you to monetize, and big enough for you to sell to others by joining the world of email affiliates. That's where there's money to be made, in selling your own products and selling for others.

Using Affiliates to Grow

Affiliates are a loosely organized, disparate group of individuals and companies, including bloggers and internet marketers, who have developed a sizable email list they'll send to on behalf of others. One hundred thousand recipients is the magic threshold for being considered a big affiliate with the potential to generate significant revenue with an email.

For us, affiliates have become the key to building our own list and generating profits. We'll use an affiliate's list to send an offer to watch our new docuseries for free. When recipients register to watch, they enter their email address in our system, and now they're on our list. We compensate the affiliates by paying them for everyone who clicks, for everyone who converts, or sometimes by commission for anything we sell the recipient.

The challenge in accessing the affiliate market is that it's a closed group. That means affiliates have plenty of options to choose from, and if you're unknown, it can be difficult to get a sizable affiliate to email for you. So, the key is to invest time in developing relationships with affiliates. People don't always do business with their friends, but when push comes to shove, they prefer to.

I foster these relationships in numerous ways, beginning with mastermind events. I don't start by asking the people I meet to email for me—you've got to give before you get. I begin by offering to mail to my list for them. With time, you'll get to be known as somebody who's in the affiliate game, and opportunities will open for you.

I also meet affiliates by receiving their emails. The best way to find out who's mailing is to sign up for lots of offers. I get a thousand emails a day, and I always try to scan them to stay on top of who's mailing what.

After building their list, affiliates have two goals in mind. The first is monetizing it by selling things to recipients that they don't produce but simply market. The second is not wearing out their list—irritating recipients with bad offers, too many offers, chasing them off in one way or another and losing their list. Their aim is the opposite of that: they're always trying to grow.

I've learned when I develop an offer not to test it with affiliates. I test it with paid traffic first—through Google ads, Facebook ads, other ads I buy, honing my offer through testing until it's highly profitable. When I go to an affiliate, that means I can tell them what they're likely to make by mailing it. If you succeed in getting a bunch of affiliates to mail for you, but the offer fails, they'll never send another email for you. This is what they do for a living, so test at your risk, not theirs.

A big affiliate can make $5,000 to $25,000 a day by sending emails. It's a business, and they treat it that way. So do I. I'll have friends approach me naïvely, asking me to email my list for them. From their point of view, it's an easy ask; "Jeff's my friend; there's no reason he won't do this for me." What they don't realize is that sending for them could mean walking away from making $5,000 to $25,000 that day. They're effectively asking me to give them thousands of dollars, just for the fun of it. That's the stark reality of the affiliate market.

Once you start emailing for others, you'll find that marketers sometimes offer rewards for the affiliate whose mailing drives the most leads. Last year the marketing gurus Tony Robbins and Dean Graziosi were promoting a free webinar, and on that webinar they sold a marketing program. The five affiliates who sent the most traffic to their webinar got to go to Tony's private island in Fiji for a private mastermind; the top affiliate got to fly there in Tony's private jet.

Even if I have zero chance of winning a prize for a big promotion, I'll sign up to mail for it. I'll also sign up for my competitor's affiliate promotions. When the promoter sends updates on the contest, they'll list the top twenty-five or fifty affiliate participants. Then I can see who's mailing for my competitors as well as the major affiliates in the space. We're always prospecting for others who might mail for us—and striving to make it as easy and successful for them as we can, writing "swipe copy" they can cut and paste, providing great tracking software, keeping them up to date on what's happening. And running our own contests too.

DROPPING PIXELS

My first goal in marketing is always to get someone's email address, and my second goal is to drop a pixel on them. We have a saying: "Pixels are people too."

Pixels are cookies, and you can drop a pixel in the browser of someone who views one of your videos or comes to your page. Facebook provides them; Google provides them. They enable you to go back and advertise to these people. This is why, when you view a product on a website, and an hour later get on Facebook, you—amazingly—see an ad for the product in your stream. It's why you see a disclaimer at the bottom of pages you visit: "This site uses cookies," and you have to click to acknowledge that you understand.

I create pixel banks related to a particular film—say it's our wine series—by putting free content online for people to watch and dropping a pixel on each of them. I may end up with two hundred thousand or three hundred thousand people who I know are interested in wine and are already familiar with my work. Instead of running an ad that reaches ten million people, I can target a much smaller audience that's likely to be highly receptive.

This is an opportunity you shouldn't miss. A filmmaker and friend once called me, looking for ways to distribute a beautiful film he had made. A snippet he had placed on

YouTube garnered 1.1 million views organically, and he was thrilled.

"Did you drop a pixel on the people who viewed it?" I asked.

His answer wasn't what I hoped for: "I don't know what that means," he said.

If you put something out there and it spreads, the fact that 1.1 million people saw it means nothing to you if you haven't prepared to capture that information. You have no way to capitalize on it, because you have no way to reach them.

TRUTH, VULNERABILITY, AND RELATIONSHIPS

Gary Halbert was one of the greatest copywriters who ever lived, and I worked with him on a couple of projects some years ago. As we were tossing around ideas, Gary told me something that has always stuck: the most valuable commodity in the world is truth. People are sick and tired of spin, from government, from politicians, from advertisers. The world is so full of lies that the single most valuable commodity is the truth, Gary said. If you really want to be successful in marketing, focus on the truth. People can feel it, and they'll resonate with it.

While it's a tactic, this commodity of truth, of openness, has become so philosophically ingrained in me that it's a way of being. The way I live in my relationships with my friends is the same way I want to be all the time with my customers. It's become so important to me that I don't treat it as a tactic. I treat it as a key value.

What's true in life is true in marketing: People are always sorting, for better and worse. They're asking themselves, Is this a valuable relationship?

We're not always good at it. I was once flying on Delta from Salt Lake to Dallas in a Lockheed L-1011: six seats in first class, in three rows of two. It was full. I was sitting in the last row in first class when I noticed this heavy guy in a suit come lumbering down the aisle in my direction. "Please go on to coach," I said to myself—but sure enough, he sat down next to me.

I didn't feel like talking with anybody, so I gave him my closed vibe for most of the flight, and he seemed fine with that. We didn't exchange a word for more than two hours. About thirty minutes outside of Dallas, he asked for a second Diet Coke. When the flight attendant brought it, she stumbled and spilled it all over his suit. He was very gracious, but she was mortified. After toweling him off, she brought him a bottle of wine, courtesy of Delta, and told him the airline would cover his dry cleaning. He thanked her, told her he didn't drink wine, and they struck up a conversation.

My ears perked up when I heard her call him "Mr. Hunt" and tell him how she'd drive by his ranch in Westlake on her way home from the airport. That's when I realized I'd been sitting next to Bunker Hunt for two hours. He and his brother were two of the richest men in the world. At the time, I was a stockbroker in my twenties who had no business shunning anybody; I'd been sitting next to the richest man in the world for two hours, busy shooting him "don't talk to me" vibes the entire trip.

I made a commitment, then and there, never to prejudge another person, ever.

But the story also points to a lesson: people are judging, always, and as a marketer, you need to be aware of it. One of the keys to success is attracting people, and to attract people it's best to be attractive yourself. There's no one better at it than pickup artists. I'm not saying I approve of their dating behavior; what I'm saying is that they've mastered the art of appearing as a high-value person.

Here's a paradox for you: I've also come to believe that once you have someone's attention and that person begins to perceive you or your company as offering something of value, being attractive alone won't lead you into a deeper relationship. What will? Honesty, vulnerability, and truth.

Dean Graziosi, an entrepreneur, investor, and bestselling author, told me that the easiest way to communicate the truth is to share the very thing you'd be embarrassed for others to know. Where people love to meet is in our vulnerabilities, in our openness. Be willing to share your sorrow, your sadness, your weakness, your vulnerabilities.

This works both ways. When we talk about marketing, my partner, Patrick, always asks the question: "What is their silent dread?" By that he means, what do the people we're trying to reach worry about in the back of their minds? The things they're not talking about with their friends?

When you can speak to someone's silent dread, they will feel understood by you, because they know you're seeing past the surface, to their real worries and fears and thoughts. One of the most successful marketing headlines of all time is only three words long: Be Taller Instantly. They were selling shoe lifts, and they did it by touching a negative emotion that all of us carry inside: "I am not enough."

Speaking from it, and speaking to it, is speaking from truth, and it's powerful.

TALKING—AND LISTENING

I've learned that your marketing doesn't end when you make a sale. You need to think of it as a conversation and follow it through. After someone buys your product, they'll start a conversation in their head. It can be anything from, "Wow! That was the smartest thing I ever did" to "Well, I hope I didn't just make a bad decision" to "How long will it take to be shipped here?" To round out your marketing, you need to stand in the shoes of your prospect and think, "What are they scared of right now? What are they hoping for? What could they use?" Offer reassurance and helpful information: "Congratulations, you just made a wonderful decision; we know how happy you're going to be, and it's shipping tomorrow." That's marketing that leads to another sale later.

With time and the right messages, conversations build toward relationships—and it's in relationships where businesses make their money. People don't refund relationships; they refund transactions. Think of your go-to restaurant in town, where the owner knows you by name, always makes you feel welcome, and pays special attention to your guest. If you happen to have a bad meal there, you don't walk out saying you'll never eat there again—and that's because of the relationship. As you structure your offers, always bear in mind building a relationship by asking yourself how you can give more value than what your customer is expecting.

WORD-OF-MOUTH MARKETING

The marketing you do isn't the only way to get customers, and it may not even be the best. Twenty-five years ago, a marketing researcher named George Silverman began doing surveys exploring people's buying decisions. He found they'd make as many as thirty to fifty small decisions along the way to their buy: "Will it be too technical for me? Will I be able to set it up? Will it be enough of an improvement?"

The one consistent thing he found came right before purchase: the recommendation of a friend. An endorsement from someone you know has a hundred times more value than the word of a professional reviewer. Think about movies; how many times have you read a reviewer skewer a new movie and gone to see it anyway because your friends were gushing about it? You'll give that much more weight.

The most important aspect of marketing is good word-of-mouth. And yet no company has a vice president of word-of-mouth. It's something we let happen, that we hope happens. We encourage it when we see it, but we don't make it a business priority to invest in word-of-mouth marketing.

It's a key leverage point. It means asking your customers for referrals and offering incentives in return. It means stimulating buzz about your offer, not in the press, but with your customers, thanking them profusely, delivering more value than they expect, offering rewards, and getting them to talk about you.

I've learned to look for every opportunity to generate word-of-mouth. This will be an invisible sales force that's in the field working for you all the time.

MARKETING AND SALES

The worlds and languages of marketing and sales overlap, but I think of them as different. Marketing is the story; sales is the ask. The job of marketing is to make sales easier. A TV ad that keeps the mattress store in town in your mind is marketing; an 800-number-buy-now ad is sales.

Remember how I told you there's no outsourcing your marketing? Now it's time for another unfortunate truth: as an entrepreneur, selling is also a skill you need to master. We're headed there next.

8

SALES

All selling is avoiding resistance.

(FROM JEFF'S NOTEBOOK)

I started my career as a documentary filmmaker by selling encyclopedias door-to-door when I was eighteen. I was so naïve that I didn't even recognize it for the crappy job that it was. But it taught me so much.

The pitch was based on reverse psychology, and it was harsh. We didn't talk about selling encyclopedias. We interviewed the people who let us inside their door to see if they were qualified for us to place an entire learning center in their home.

"Before I tell you about this," I'd say, "I need to ask a few questions about education. Do you care about your children's education? Do you feel education is important?" On and on it went.

"Well," I'd say, "the reason I asked you these questions is we're looking for families to place an entire learning center in their home, all at the cost of the daily newspaper. The way

I qualify a family is by their reactions to what I show them. Would you like to see the learning center? Would you like to see if you qualify?"

They'd say yes. I'd pause and give them a good look, as if I were making up my mind. "Tell you what," I'd say. "I'm going to go outside for my briefcase and bring it in and show you the learning center."

It's called a qualification pitch. We never shifted strategy all the way through to a purchase. It was critical that I never become a salesman trying to sell them encyclopedias; instead, I was a representative of the company there to see if they qualified for a learning center. It's a powerful and effective tool; you have to keep your moral compass, because it can be used for bad as easily as for good.

Back to pickup artists for a moment: They use a technique they call "negging," where they'll identify the leader in a group of girls—usually the most attractive—and say something negative about her in front of the others. "Wow, does she always talk this much?" That sends a new dynamic rippling through the group: wait a minute, he's not sold.

Of course, I was knocking on doors hoping to sell encyclopedias, not picking up girls. I'd sit Mr. and Mrs. Jones on the couch in their living room, and I'd have each of them hold a corner of the posters I unfolded. "Do you like that, Mr. Jones?" I'd say after explaining a poster. "Can you see where that's important, Mrs. Jones?" All the way through the pitch, I'd ask them to commit over and over: yes, yes, yes.

Before I got to my closing question, I'd explain all the bonuses they got, and how the price of $699 amounted to only twenty-five cents a day (fifty cents on Sunday) over ten years. Then I'd deliver the line: "I don't think that's just fair; I think it's way more than fair. But how does that sound to you, Mr. Jones? Mrs. Jones?"

If they didn't bite, I had one more card to play: "I'll tell you what I'm going to do, Mr. and Mrs. Jones. I'm going to start packing my briefcase, and if you stop me before I get out the door, I'll be happy to recommend you for this purchase. If not, it's been a pleasure meeting you." I'd pack up, and I wouldn't say another word until I walked out the door.

There was nothing I liked better than making a sale. But a close second was walking out on someone who couldn't make a decision. No arguing with them, no trying to talk them into it. I'd just dust off my feet and walk to the next door. Because what mattered most was the attitude of the person making the sales pitch: me.

WHAT'S CHANGED, AND WHAT HASN'T

Selling has been around as long as there have been people. I remember reading an old sales book by Elmer Wheeler, who trained salesmen back in the early 1900s to go knock on the back door, not the front. The woman of the house would look him over through the screen door.

"Ma'am," he'd say, "I'd like to—" and then she'd mop her brow. If she didn't, he'd mop his brow. "How would you like it," he'd say, "if I could make your kitchen fifteen degrees cooler?"

Because she was in there baking bread—and the guy knocking on her door was a bread salesman. "Let me do your baking for you, and we won't have your oven heating up your whole house."

So many products in the old days were sold door-to-door. Garbage disposals. Vacuum cleaners. And learning centers.

We don't see many door-to-door salespeople anymore. Sales has grown more sophisticated—but people are still people, and that will never change. We're driven by the same basic desires, the need to be recognized or the need to be appreciated; we all struggle with the same basic fears and insecurities, the things we're afraid that we might be. These are the buttons that we push, ethically, to make people want our product.

THE FIVE ESSENTIALS

The trainer who taught me the art of selling door-to-door said there were five essentials to the job. Number one was enthusiasm. Second, walk fast. Third, shake hands firmly. Number four, make strong eye contact. Fifth: smile. Five essentials, he'd say, but only one was key: enthusiasm. If you had it, you didn't need to remember the other four. Because if you're enthusiastic, you would walk fast. If you're enthusiastic, you shake hands firmly. If you're enthusiastic, you make great eye contact.

This strange introduction to working life taught me psychology. Maybe the husband was the head of the family, but the wife was the neck—and the neck could turn the head side to side or up and down. More important, selling encyclopedias made me immune to rejection. It wasn't the last house that mattered; it was the next one. It taught me to endure. We once worked six months straight without a single day off. By the time I was nineteen, I had been in literally thousands of houses, meeting thousands of people, talking about something I wanted to sell them. And I had earned enough to buy a Cadillac.

From time to time I still have nightmares where I go broke and have to resort to selling door-to-door. It's nothing I ever want to do again. But it was the experience of a lifetime.

DAVID'S WISDOM
EVERY SCOUT AN EAGLE SCOUT

David was a Mormon, active in the Church of Jesus Christ of Latter-day Saints, and until recently, the LDS church was the biggest supporter of Boy Scouts in the country. The church wove scouting into its programs. And one year, David was called to serve as the scoutmaster.

David being David, he set out to do something unprecedented, something extraordinary: he wanted every one of the thirty-three boys who were eligible to be Eagle Scouts to achieve that goal that year— 100 percent—and he did it.

It was his windmill, and like Don Quixote, he attacked it. His commitment was 100 percent, hands on, all in, on behalf of the boys. He'd drive to their houses to pick them up for a meeting. He labored to make sure every one of them earned their merit badges.

> He inspired each to reach for the goal he defined for
> them—and they did it.
>
> That's sales at its best.

BELIEF IN THE VALUE

Timidity stops many people from marketing. Overcoming
it begins with understanding—and believing in—the value
of your proposition. If what you're offering is valuable, if it
delivers something unique in the marketplace, if people are
better off when they buy it, then you're literally harming
them if you don't do your very best to convince them that
it's the right choice for them—if it is. If it's not, you need to
be selling something else. And if you go out and do all the
marketing but don't ask for the order, then all you're doing
is the heavy lifting for your competitors. Within yourself
and within your company, you've got to find the boldness
required not only to do the marketing but to ask for the
order and get the money.

You can't communicate value without creating a sense
of appreciation. In my twenties, when I had the company
that sold water softeners in home visits, the salesman would
go with test kits that contained a miniature water softener.
They'd find a dirty spot on the oven, or a pan with stubborn
grime, and demonstrate how much easier it was to clean
with soft water. They'd show how much further shampoo
went with soft water. By the time they finished their demo,
the value of that water treatment system was way higher in
the customer's mind than what it cost. "If you're going to sell

a $2,000 water softener," the sales trainer would always say, "you've got to give a $10,000 presentation." Once a customer can see and understand the value of good, clean, conditioned water, then the price is ridiculously good.

When I first became a stockbroker, I went to work at a tiny brokerage in Dallas. They'd done an IPO on a company whose main product was a trailer that folded up and went in the trunk. It was called Trailer in a Trunk, and it was a stupid idea, but the brokerage firm had taken them public. It was made very clear to us that our job was to move a lot of Trailer in a Trunk stock. It was a slog. I was beating my head against the wall. Clients didn't believe it would do well, and what's worse, neither did I.

I stopped selling Trailer in a Trunk and started selling IBM and Microsoft, great companies I could believe in. If you don't believe in what you're selling, you can't be effective selling it. If you can't sell things you believe in where you are, you need to go somewhere else. It's that critical.

GETTING IN STEP

A key to selling is to join the conversation that's already occurring in your customer's head. There has never been a better demonstration of this than marketing during the coronavirus pandemic. With the pandemic at its height, I'd get emails from companies promoting their biggest sale of the year, 20 percent off designer jeans. When the conversation going on in most people's heads is about buying toilet paper, telling them you're running a 20 percent discount on jeans is not going to be successful.

Elmer Wheeler, the old sales guru of the early 1900s, called it "getting in step" with people.

Think about the times you've been walking on the street in New York City or Las Vegas where there are lots of people on every corner trying to hand you circulars. They typically stand in your way, making you feel like a linebacker trying to push your way through the other team's blockers. I avoid them like the plague. But every now and then, one of them will spot me and, instead of getting in the way, follow and walk with me. When someone is in step with you, it's much harder to break away.

When you're selling, don't stand in front of someone and stop them to make your pitch; turn and walk beside them, then start the conversation. And instead of trying to start a new conversation, talk to them about the conversations they're already having: their fears, their desires, their secret impulses.

Don't stop walking with them after they've bought, either. Remind them that they're doing a smart thing. Show them your Better Business Bureau badge on your order page. Let them know someone else just bought the same thing. If you're in sales, you're always selling.

FEEL, FELT, FOUND

It's one of the oldest sales formulas around: feel, felt, found. It's an approach to answering objections, first taught to insurance agents in the 1920s. Whenever I see or hear it, I laugh, and I see and hear it a lot in good marketing. There are different ways to express it, but it's a way of joining someone where they are: "I know how you feel; I felt the same way myself. However, when I learned X, here's what I found." You're not trying to change their thinking; you're trying to join it, build a rapport, and guide it forward. "I know how you feel about gizmos; I felt the same way. But once I got *this* gizmo, here's what I found."

AVOIDING RESISTANCE

If a friend gives you a hug, you'll hug them back, and it feels good. Human contact! But if your friend holds you tight and doesn't let go, sooner or later it becomes uncomfortable, and you start to resist it: "Hey, dude, let go." If he continues to hold on, your resistance will build until you literally push the hugger away.

Anyone who has raised teenagers has learned to avoid resistance. It's a perfect laboratory for learning how to create and how to avoid resistance. The phrase we used is, "steering the horse in the direction that it's going." If you don't want your kids to do something, telling them not to do it is the wrong way to go about it.

I remember when one of my sons was eighteen, he had a life decision that we really wanted him to make. I knew not to push him in the direction I thought best—even though he was consistently saying: "I don't want that direction for my life. I'm not going to do that."

My wife would always want to jump in and argue with him.

I'd say: "Let it go, just leave it. Let that statement just sit there."

Finally, after about six months, he came in, sat down, and said: "You know what? I think I've changed my mind. I think I want to do it."

My wife almost jumped out of her chair, but I shook my head. It was just bait. He was waiting for us to say, "Oh, we're so glad you've come to your senses!" Then he would resist it. I had to force myself to be neutral: "Well, these are big decisions. It's your life. Just know that we want the best for you, and we support you in whatever you decide to do." By giving him nothing to resist, he was able to come to the correct decision.

How does that relate to sales? Think about how many times you've been in a conversation and realized all of a sudden, "Wait, they're trying to sell me something." As soon as that thought strikes, you resist.

Everything in your selling, like everything in your marketing, has to be about avoiding resistance in your client, and not generating it. Keep their best interest in mind. Don't be the friend who hugs too hard for too long.

That's just good human dynamics—and that's the topic we'll turn to next.

9

THE HUMAN ELEMENT

*Don't lead by catching employees doing something
wrong. Lead by catching them doing something right.*

(FROM JEFF'S NOTEBOOK)

The biggest restriction on any business is people. It's
not technology, it's not capital, it's not regulation
or any of the other constricting elements that businesses face. Almost any business could be two, five, ten
times larger if they could hire more people, better people,
the right people, and create a culture where they thrive. But
entrepreneurs share some unique characteristics that can
make them hard to work with. Overcoming this is a key to
survival, a key to growth, and a key to not blowing up your
team again and again.

If you can get this part right, you can get almost everything else wrong. I'd even go further: if you're in the wrong
business but have the right people, you'll eventually find
the right business. Let's talk about some of the lessons I've
learned in succeeding through the people who work for you.

RIGHT TEAM, RIGHT TIME

My first hire when I started a business was once a brilliant, young graphic designer. We would sit and work into the night creating the materials to take the idea in my head and put it in visual form to share with the people who would become investors or employees. The kid was smart, and I enjoyed working with him so much.

The company started to grow, and he was a big part of it. I brought him with me to every meeting and his feedback was great. For a young guy, he had tremendous wisdom.

In time the company raised millions of dollars, and we did what companies do as they mature. We created a formal board and put management in place. That changed the dynamics. It became inappropriate for the company's graphic designer to attend all these management meetings.

I watched his sadness. He went from having complete access and involvement to being shut out. Finally, he became disillusioned and quit. I can't blame him at all. But you have to recognize this as the natural progression in the growth of a business.

When we plan a military invasion, the first troops in are the Special Forces. They don't look or act much like soldiers. They have beards, they have long hair, they reject standard military routines. But they're fearless improvisers, and they do the work of two or three or ten regular soldiers. They go in first and seize the critical objectives.

Then we send in the troops. They're in larger groups, they're disciplined, they're tightly regulated, and they usually don't get along very well with the Special Forces.

They're followed by the occupying forces, the adminis-
trative types. They stay, they bring order to chaos, and they
don't get along with the previous two teams.

I hate to use this battle metaphor, but it illustrates a
business reality: for your company to grow, you need to
know which team to put on the field at which time. As your
business matures, many of your start-up employees may not
survive going to the next level. Not every employee in a
maturing company will be a star or needs to be. I once did
a project with Microsoft and was stunned by the number of
mediocre employees.

The team you'll need to start your business is different
from the team you'll need to grow it. To scale, you need
mediocre employees—which goes against the common
thinking that you succeed by building a team of superstars.
You cannot scale with superstars. It's just not the way the
world works, because there are only so many superstars. A
Navy SEAL is the best of the best of the best, but you can't
build an entire military out of elite, first-in troops. Certainly
you want to hire the best people you can, but sooner rather
than later you're going to have to figure out how to succeed with people who are not superstars. That's reality. I've
found over and over that the Pareto principle applies to your
employees: the top 20 percent of people are responsible for
80 percent of the output, and at the same time the bottom 20
percent are responsible for 80 percent of headaches.

I've previously mentioned the business I built in my twenties: five distributorships that sold water softeners in Texas. A
farm girl named Pam Helm joined our team as a salesperson.
Soon there were weeks when Pam, by herself, would outsell

my entire sales force of a dozen to fifteen. She was a phenom-enon. We worked on Saturdays, and on one of those days Pam came into the office to write a couple of orders. She told me she had a couple more appointments that night.

"Pam," I said, "you've worked hard all week. Why don't you take Saturday night off?"

She shook her head no. "Jeff, I feel so guilty when I don't work Saturday night!" she said.

Everyone recognized how strong she was. We had a single assigned parking space at our office building, where I used to park. Then it occurred to me that I should be parking out back, so we painted "top salesman" on the spot, and I announced to the team that whoever had the most sales would get the honor of parking there every week. The response was quiet enough that I heard one of the guys in the room mutter under his breath, "I don't care where she parks."

I would have loved to have fifteen Pam Helms on my team. But I didn't. I had one. And I wouldn't have had a business if I didn't have a team of twelve to fifteen. By defi-nition, most were mediocre—average—and so the challenge I faced was learning how to get the most out of them too.

IT'S NOT THEM; IT'S YOU

Maybe you're familiar with the Enneagram Personality Test and the nine personality types it identifies. Entrepreneurs are often Type Eights—the "challenger." One of the nega-tive characteristics of a Type Eight is the tendency to blame others. They'll walk through the business and say: "Wait, who did this? Who made that decision?" At the time, that fit me. It's probably the most damaging thing you can do to your team. It makes them scared to move in any direction, for fear of being second-guessed.

The water softener business ran off of a big phone room in each city that spent its days making leads for our sales-people. Then I and the sales managers in our other cities held a meeting with the salespeople at four o'clock every afternoon. We'd train and teach and motivate, and then at five o'clock the salespeople headed out to make their calls. I spent my nights dispatching leads, and if a salesperson had trouble closing a sale, they'd put the customer on the phone with me.

I was running the office in Waco, Texas, where we prob-ably had fifteen or twenty people—and they just weren't productive. I was mad at them. I didn't feel like there was one winner in the whole group.

One of my early mentors owned the factory that made the water softener that we sold. His name was Lowell Foletta, and he had come up through direct sales. Lowell was a brilliant motivator, a walking ball of enthusiasm and positivity.

I called him and said: "Lowell, our sales are down, and I'm ticked off. I've got a lousy team."

"Jeff," Lowell said, "you can fire everybody and start all over if you want. But I'll make you a bet. You give me your losers, your crummy team that you're wanting to fire. You go get all new people and train all new people, and I'll bet you my office in Phoenix against yours in Waco that we'll outsell you.

"It's not the speed of the crew," he told me. "The speed of the crew is the speed of the boss."

I knew the second he said it that if Lowell took my losers, he would make them better. He would train them. He would motivate them. The problem wasn't them; the problem was me.

I didn't take him up on the bet. Instead, I recognized the need to shift my mindset from placing blame to taking responsibility. The question wasn't "Who should I fire first?" but "What do I have to do to ensure success?" I doubled down on training and motivation in ways big and small.

We put a bell on the desk of every telemarketer in the phone room, and every time they made an appointment for a salesperson they'd ring their bell. We might have fifteen telemarketers in a room, and the goal was for bells to be ringing for the whole time they were on the phone.

When our salespeople came in for our daily meeting at four o'clock, we'd have them answer a series of questions for every sale on a one-page form. *How did you get the lead? What did the house look like? What questions did the people ask and how did you answer them? What happened when you asked for the order? Did you use any closers?*

In our meeting, they'd tell the story of the sale. Someone new would always raise a hand and say, "I tried that last night and it didn't work." I had to shut them down. We don't train on failure stories, I'd say; we train on success stories. We faxed the stories between our offices so everyone could build on our successes.

We put a magnetic whiteboard on the wall in every office with every salesperson's name down one side and every day of the week across the top. Every presentation got a red star. Every sale got a dollar sign. Everyone who walked into the office could see the success or failure of everyone on the team. Everyone could see who was performing, who wasn't, and what was possible. We began contests between offices: whoever wrote the most orders that night got pizza, and the loser pays. We ran monthly and weekly contests, tracking progress on a board everyone could see. Some days one team got on a speakerphone during the sales meeting, called the other, and shouted that they were going to kick the other team's collective butt.

Every few months, we'd buy hundreds of balloons for the office. We'd insert a piece of paper with a number on it—$1, $2, $5, $10, $25, or $100—in each balloon, blow it up, and tie it off. (No, we weren't crazy; there were way more $1, $2, and $5 slips than the big prizes!) We hung a big net from the ceiling with all the balloons in it. When someone hit a goal or came up with a good idea, we'd give them a balloon pop; a great idea or a really big month and they'd get three. They might win $1, $25, even $100. We'd pay them on the spot, in cash, right there.

We began to do group hirings, running blind ads in the newspaper that brought a hundred people in for a group interview. I had our salespeople come, and after I made my presentation, each of the salespeople stood to talk about what working with us had meant to them. My goal was helping us hire—but in time I realized I was reaping another, bigger benefit from these testimonials: they were forcing our salespeople to realize how grateful they were for their jobs.

The truth is that it was a *very* difficult job. This experience taught me that the harder the job, the more emotional support you as the boss need to provide. Our sales surged as I learned to take responsibility for that. I got back far more in motivation than I invested in training time, newspaper ads, and balloon pops.

I used to say that responsibility leads to power. Now I see a more direct connection: responsibility *is* power. The most powerful person in a company is usually the CEO, and they're the most powerful because they have the most responsibility. Anytime you shirk responsibility—and blame is the easiest tool for that—you lose power. Anytime you need to gain power over a situation, take responsibility. Blame gets you nowhere.

GETTING DOWN ON THE SHOP FLOOR

Back in the nineties, I owned a company called Capstone Entertainment in Salt Lake City that made family-friendly films. We employed almost three hundred telemarketers. They sold the films over the phone, using telephone lists that we bought. We used an active dialer computer program that would anticipate when someone was about to hang up and start dialing the next number in advance. The telemarketer would hang up and, literally, ten to fifteen seconds later, they'd be on the phone with someone else. No dialing. No pauses.

It was a stressful job. Turnover was high. We ran help-wanted ads in the newspaper every week. We devoted a large human resources department to hiring and training new people. I used to joke that I wasn't the biggest employer in Salt Lake; I was the biggest ex-employer.

It worked. Barely. It was a struggle to hire and sell fast enough, and if we didn't change something, we were in danger of going out of business. I hired a consultant to look at how we could make sales more efficient. He did something that I had never done. He sat in a cubicle on the marketing floor, plugged into the computer, and listened to the telemarketers, one by one, for two solid days. On the third day, he came back with a recommendation.

I was really humiliated. I'd owned the business for a year or two, and the one thing I had never done was listen to my salespeople on the phone with my customers. I read reports about them, I talked to management about them, but I'd never done the work of actually sitting and listening to them. My office was on the third floor, sales was on the first. All the information I needed to make my business more efficient was down on that sales floor and had been available to me all that time, just two floors away.

His recommendation came out of left field. Whenever someone bought a film, we asked for referrals: "Who else should we call and talk to about family-friendly films?" He noticed that the referrals were five to seven times more likely to buy than any of the best phone numbers we could purchase. Instead of only asking people who bought for referrals, he suggested that we also ask for referrals from people who didn't buy: "Okay, well, who else should we call? Who do you think might be interested?"

It turned out that, in order to get off the phone without buying, people gave us names. We got massive numbers of referrals. It was very productive. To cover our costs, each of our salespeople had to sell an average of three films every two hours. On referrals, they sold seven to ten.

The consultant had given us a great recommendation—but it came with a warning: the penalty for making this change would be even more turnover. It's a hard job calling strangers on the phone. For our telemarketers, gathering referrals from people who didn't buy was an additional stress point. Some were already feeling all the stress they could handle, and this was too much. Turnover rose from 7 percent a week to 10 percent.

We could run ads and hire about thirty people a week. But with a telemarketing staff of three hundred and turnover of 10 percent, we were maxed out. We couldn't grow, because we could only hire as many salespeople as we lost each week.

The lesson for me in this—and for entrepreneurs—is that you have to measure the stress that your employees feel. And you have to counteract it.

The first thing I did was to put a popcorn machine in the office. Free popcorn, on demand. Then we began bringing caterers in at lunchtime, offering fresh hot food to the team on the sales floor that day. Each step we took was intended to alleviate the stress of the job we were asking our employees to do.

We didn't eliminate turnover. Calling strangers on the phone was still a hard job. But we tipped the turnover balance in our favor. The telemarketing staff grew, and so did sales.

As entrepreneurs, we often attempt the impossible. It's part of who we are. But when we ask the same of our employees, they pay a price—which means that, in the end, we do too. I've learned the importance of walking in their shoes and seeing the world as they do, not the way I imagine it to be. It's work, but I've learned that I need to do it.

Years ago I had the opportunity to interview the dean of the Columbia University Graduate School of Journalism, a woman named Joan Konner, for a project on women's leadership.

The secret to her success? "I do windows," she said. Working at an elite university, she was surrounded by people who felt that, metaphorically, washing windows was beneath them. She succeeded by jumping in and washing them.

I once heard Lowell Foletta, a mentor I mentioned earlier in this chapter, make the same point in a different way while addressing a business group. "What kind of person are you?" he asked his audience. "The kind who walks into a living room and steps over a dirty diaper, or the kind that picks it up and puts it away?" I had a couple of kids in diapers at the time, and the honest answer is that I was probably just another guy who would step over the dirty diaper and leave it for my wife to pick up. After he posed the question, I was never able to do that again. If I drive into the garage and see something that's fallen from the trash can onto the floor, I hear Lowell's voice in my head. There's a 0 percent chance I'll walk into the house without picking it up. If you can develop the mentality to do what needs to be done 100 percent of the time, you'll do it at the right time.

HIRING SLOW, FIRING FAST

Experience has taught me that I am the very worst person to do the hiring for my companies. The salesman in me kicks in. I can't help it. I'd be interviewing somebody, supposedly to find out if they were someone I should hire, and I would spend 80 percent of our time together talking instead of listening. I wasn't comfortable asking hard questions, and I felt the need to sell them on the job. It was as if my role was talking the candidate into letting me hire them. Meanwhile, I wasn't doing the work of finding out if they were the right person for the job.

Entrepreneurs are salespeople. If that describes you, hiring is something that's better outsourced to somebody on your team or someone you bring in for that purpose. I've worked with one such outsider who could drill deep and get great information—stuff I just wasn't capable of learning on my own.

I've learned that speed in hiring is not your friend. The easiest way to avoid the pain of firing people is to slow down the hiring. It's much like managing your commitments. The best way to stop breaking commitments is to go upstream and make fewer commitments in the first place. People say yes to potential hires too easily. You have to learn to say no.

There are a couple of benefits to this. When you make the hiring process a bit of an ordeal, you're testing the resolve of the candidates and seeing for yourself, through their behavior, how they deal with uncertainty and disappointment. You'll also reduce turnover, because research has shown that the harder it is to get a job, the harder it is to leave it.

When I say "ordeal," I'm not talking about asking candidates to walk over a bed of hot coals or anything like that. It's become common for tech companies to ask applicants to make a video explaining why they'd be great for the job—a terrific test of creativity. Companies will ask developers to demonstrate their thought process, their skills, and the compatibility of their approach by taking a coding test. Entrepreneurial companies will incorporate a writing assignment into the hiring process, because almost all jobs in that environment require communication skills. I've also found there's value in having the members of the team who would work with the applicants interview them, individually and as a group. From the company's perspective, it's all good for the hiring perspective; from the perspective of the person being hired, it's a bit of an ordeal. But the benefits work in both directions, because the applicant learns too: "Are these people I want to work with?"

Still, sometimes, in the end, you are going to have to fire someone. No one likes to do it. But most of the business pain that I've had has come from firing way too slow.

I've heard Brian Tracy, an author and business coach, say that the best time to fire someone is the first time you think about it, that everything else is just pain. I find that extreme but it's a great reminder, and it has increased the speed with which I fire people, but I don't take it literally.

I've embraced a business rule I learned from Kat Merritt, a director who runs our companies: If we're profitable, you can have one "project." That's somebody you believe in but who isn't doing a good job. If you're making money, you can invest in helping that person improve. But if you're on investor money, you're not even allowed one project. That discipline helps. I've run companies where I had numerous projects at the same time, people who weren't doing the job that I needed them to do. But I was emotionally tied to them, or I cared about them, or I didn't want to go through the pain of letting them go. That's a mistake. It will drag you down. And in the end, they'll be better off in a different role somewhere else.

DAVID'S WISDOM
INSPECT WHAT YOU EXPECT

David once invested a lot of money in one of my companies, and I was embarrassed to call him with a bad report: We had failed to hit one of our milestones. We'd had a technical problem and wasted time and money because of a bad decision by one of our employees. I started describing this to him when David interrupted.

"Jeff," he said, "is it human error?"

I said yes, and that was all he needed to hear.

"I got it," he said. "You're always going to have human error—but, Jeff, you've got to inspect what you expect."

That's become one of my driving principles. Employees are going to make mistakes, and there's nothing you can do about it. The worst thing you can do is to hang over their shoulder and try to stop the

mistakes from happening. You need to delegate. You
need to trust. And you need to check in periodically, to
make sure they're doing what you expected.

You've got to inspect what you expect.

BUILDING THE RIGHT TEAM FOR *YOU*

One of the biggest mistakes I've made in the past is surrounding myself with people who are just like me because
I like them. We share the same interests, the same way of
thinking, and we enjoy one another's company. But that also
means we make the same mistakes. Experience has taught
me to surround myself with people who possess the qualities
I *don't* bring to the table.

If there's a spectrum between action-oriented doers with
great follow-through and visionary thinkers, you'll find me
at the thinking end of that scale. I have a prejudice toward
thinking, and I've learned that I can't succeed without surrounding myself with people who have a prejudice toward
doing.

I once hired an assistant who was further down the
action scale than anyone I'd ever met. One day, when she
walked into my office, I greeted her with, "Hey, I've got
something I need you to do."

She answered with "You got it!" and took three steps
toward the door before she turned around and looked at me
sheepishly. "Okay," she said. "What is it?" She may have
made more mistakes than anybody I'd ever worked with—
but she also accomplished fifty times more than anybody

I'd ever worked with. To succeed together, I had to inspect what I expect, as David Nemelka put it, trusting her to do the job while checking in—and together, playing to each of our strengths, we got so much done.

With an entrepreneurial brain, I can see the big picture and describe a vision. That alone gets me nowhere unless I surround myself with people who act fast, who are detail-oriented, who lock onto their to-do list and follow through to completion. If I surround myself with people like me, we'll just steer ourselves in circles until we drive off the edge of the cliff together, talking about the big picture all the way down.

The football great Fran Tarkenton had a saying: "You got to wrestle the bear all the way to the ground." I used to feel deficient, because that wasn't me. But I've learned I don't need to pin the bear. I'm the guy who provokes the bear; what I need is the right team around me to wrestle it to the ground.

MOVING TOWARD ABUNDANCE

Every employee relationship falls into one of three levels: rip-off, transactional, or abundance.

If employees are not doing the job that you hired them for, if they're not fulfilling the work you need them to do, they're ripping you off. If you allow your employee relationships to descend into rip-off, it's your fault, not theirs. You have to either correct them or fire them. Otherwise they'll bleed you. You can't let your people rip you off.

A transactional relationship is in balance. If you go into a car dealer, negotiate a price, and hand over the money, the dealer gives you the car. That's a transactional relationship. Nobody owes anyone anything. It's fair, and both parties benefit.

Moving that relationship to abundance from the dealer standpoint doesn't have to cost money. It doesn't mean the dealer has to throw in a car bra for nothing. It can be simpler than that. You walk in the door after you bought the car, and the salesperson greets you by name: "Hey, Jeff, it's good to see you." Somebody brings you a cup of coffee. The service manager walks over and says: "Hey, how's that new Audi running? You bring it in, we'll get that oil change done for you." These aren't things they owe you. You bought the car, so they're beyond the boundaries of a transactional relationship. These are simple things the dealer can do to move your relationship to abundance.

Your goal with employees is to never let them descend into rip-off, to insist that your relationship is at least transactional and to look for ways you can move that relationship into abundance. Popcorn machines, lunches, balloon pops. Tech companies are well known for their bean bag chairs and pool tables—when I visited Twitter's New York headquarters a couple of years ago, they even had beer on tap. Small things that make a big difference.

Of course, what makes a difference to you isn't what really matters; it's what makes a difference to your employees. At a tech company I owned, we once fell behind on our development calendar. My answer was to offer a $20,000 bonus to three key developers; the money was theirs if they could just push the project across the finish line on time. One of the best of them quit the next day. I was stunned. Where did I go wrong?

The truth is that the developers were so good, they could have gone anywhere and made more money. They were working on our project because it had meaning for them. My mistake was motivating them with money, which I wanted, and not meaning, which they wanted.

I went to the developer and told him I had misread the situation, that I'd ignored his language while speaking mine, that I was wrong, and that I valued his contributions. The result? He stayed.

INSTALLING A STRONG CULTURE

Your culture starts from the top down. It reflects your philosophy and flows from the rules you install: *We don't talk to customers like that. We don't talk to one another like that. We respond to our emails.* You have to choose the culture you want, and you have to implement it.

Once your culture is in place, it works from the bottom up. It starts to police itself, because your employees know it and protect it: *That's not the way we do it here.*

A strong culture is like an invisible hand that guides your entire company. It's your policies and procedures come to life.

I think of it as the Bernoulli effect for business. Named for an Italian physicist, this is the dynamic that causes airplanes to fly. Their wings are shaped so the air flows faster over the top than underneath, effectively creating a cell of low pressure above the wing that effectively vacuums the plane up into the air.

I saw the same dynamic lift the team at Podfitness, the fitness company I'd founded. In the beginning we hired fitness people. We put a gym in our office, and people began working out. We put a gas grill on a big patio out back, and most people grilled their own vegetables and meat for lunch. It was, quite literally, a healthy culture. As we grew, we began hiring people from all walks of life, in customer service, in our business office, in software development—people who had no personal investment in fitness but were essential to our growth. Within a month, I began to see these people change their habits. Instead of pizza, they brought salad for lunch; instead of coffee, they drank tea. They even began to use the gym. They were being vacuumed up into the culture—the Bernoulli effect of dieting.

Once you start looking for it, you'll see it everywhere in successful businesses—and you'll also notice its absence.

There's a Ruth's Chris Steak House I know, and for the longest time it was great. But a few years ago, when I had the occasion to return once or twice, it was a disappointment. If not for a business gathering at the hotel where it was situated, I might never have gone back—but there I was, a prisoner at the hotel, and I had no choice but to eat there on successive days. And it was back: spectacular service, terrific food. On the third day, I asked the server, what happened?

"Oh," she said, "I'm so glad. The previous manager just didn't care, and they replaced him with someone who did!" The standards the managers set through their own behavior created a culture; one sucked it down, while the other lifted it up.

MEASURING WHAT YOU SAY

A man says to his wife, "Honey, you look nice tonight," and she bursts into tears. Somehow he has hurt her feelings—we've all done it in some way to someone we care for. We get the opposite response we're looking for. And now we're mad at them for not getting it.

One of the presuppositions of neuro-linguistic programming (discussed in Chapter 1) is that the meaning of your communication is the response it elicits. Instead of blaming the person receiving the communication for not receiving what was intended, the communicator has to take responsibility for the response.

Whether you're dealing with employees, your kids, or your spouse, you need to take responsibility for your communication. An employee once called me out for how often I'd responded to him with, "That's the stupidest idea I've ever heard."

I argued with him: "I would never say that to someone!"

And then I heard myself say it to somebody else—"That's the stupidest idea I've ever heard." I meant it in a lighthearted way. I was just trying to set the topic aside and move on. I didn't mean it as the acid-barbed phrase that it is. It's funny. I recently watched a documentary about Bill Gates—and he's famous for saying the exact same thing to his employees. He justified it the same way I did: "I didn't really mean it."

These are the kinds of things momentum entrepreneurs can say without paying attention to the effect their words have on the people to whom they're talking.

You have to install a governor. The meaning of your communication is the response it elicits. Slow down, look at the person with whom you're speaking, read their response. There's probably no one who would enjoy hearing, "That's the stupidest idea I've ever heard!"

Embracing Disagreement

I've learned that this "stupidest idea ever!" habit of entrepreneurs does more than undermine the confidence of the people you're depending on for success. It also stops them from having the courage to disagree with you.

Experience has taught me the value of a culture in which I have to argue hard for my ideas, where we all recognize that none of us is as smart as all of us. I like it when an idea has to survive the hot anvil of debate. I will argue passionately for my ideas, and I want my team to argue against me just as passionately if they believe that I'm wrong. Because the truth is, I'm wrong as often as I'm right.

A few years ago, we interviewed Nadine Strossen, who at the time was president of the American Civil Liberties Union. She described how she often walked into rooms where she was hated before she spoke her first word, where the others in the room disagreed with the ACLU at a visceral level. She would begin by saying, "Listen, you disagree with the ACLU. Join the club. You should be at our board meetings! We never agree on anything." By doing so, she welcomed the disagreement. What could have been a fight became a discussion, a debate.

THINK WHO, NOT HOW

I can't tell you how many times I've walked into a meeting with, "Hey, I had a great idea!" I'd start thinking out loud, and I'd get enthusiastic, and we'd begin fleshing it out. Then I'd walk out of the room, think about it more, realize there were fifteen things wrong with it, and walk back into the room a few hours later to find that my team was already building a project I'd reconsidered. What to me was musing, to them was marching orders.

You have to protect your team from your ideas.

The key to that is changing the question you ask when you have your next idea.

It's not "How am I going to do this?"

It's not how, but who: "Who is going to do this?"

I have so many ideas that a business coach once refused to let me start a new project until I answered the who question. It taught me to keep a book of all my new ideas—and I could only introduce them once each quarter. That meant my idea had to survive in my notebook. Then it had to survive the hot anvil of the quarterly idea meeting. If it survived both of those obstacles, the next question wasn't how to do it, but who was going to do it.

Everybody talks about how the smart move is to have multiple streams of income. My business coach redirected me: It's not multiple streams of income, but multiple teams of income. That's how you scale, by building teams of income.

It's become very efficient for me to make three or four documentaries at the same time, even though it costs me $15,000 a day to fly my crew in and film somewhere. Let's say I'm taking a crew into Austin to film an interview for a particular project. I will look at the other series that I'm doing, and while I'm there I may film one interview on relationships, another on investing, and a third on health care—all in the same trip. Once that footage gets in, I farm it out to the producers working on different projects. I'm leveraging a single film crew, but I'm not flooding a single set of editors with all the projects I'm working on at the same time. Instead, I've learned to create teams of income.

Less Is More

I've learned that one key to creating multiple teams of income is to double down on the winners and kill the losers. We released four docuseries last year, and one was four times more successful than the others. A business coach named Scott Haldeman pointed to that success and said, "Why not do another project on that topic?" I was embarrassed that it took someone else to offer that simple suggestion. Because we'd just done a film on that topic, I had crossed it off my list. If we didn't seize on our own success, a competitor would—so, why not us? Once you've built your teams of income, feed the projects that win and starve the losers.

CELEBRATING VICTORIES

One difficulty that people have working for an entrepreneur is that we run on momentum and rarely take time to celebrate victories. Imagine you set a high goal for your sales team, and they hit it. They feel like they've finished the race and they want to catch their breath. The entrepreneur thinks: "What are you talking about? Now we can really grow!" We immediately press harder, set higher goals. We forget to celebrate our victories.

I've written before about Patrick Byrne (see Chapters 3 and 4), the founder of Overstock. He was the subject of an article in the *New Yorker* in 2020 that described this tendency in him. "Every time we felt like we had made some progress, it was never enough," a former colleague was quoted as saying. "It was that feeling of being on a treadmill."

I've actually started a Google doc that I've titled "Wins." It helps me remember to just take a minute and celebrate all our victories, even the little ones, every day. Entrepreneurs are forward thinkers—we live in the future—but we need to look back at each day with gratitude and acknowledge the wins. You may not want to slow down, you may not need to catch your breath, but your team does. Don't fight it. Lead the celebration.

CHERISHING THE REALLY IMPORTANT HUMANS

I have a good friend named Garrett Gunderson who is a financial consultant and a *New York Times* bestselling author. He grew up in a little coal mining town named Price, Utah, and he was a prodigy there. He started successful businesses when he was in high school, managing money for family members when he was still a teenager. For a young kid in a coal mining town, Garrett was extraordinary. He ended up writing a bestseller on investing titled *Killing Sacred Cows* and built a huge following. He succeeded at a high level in every aspect of his professional life.

One day Garrett was driving his Bentley back to Price to see his family. His wife was in the car with him, and she said: "You know, Garrett, you're good or great at everything you do. You're a great writer. You're a great businessperson, you're a great investor, you're a great friend. But the truth is you're only a mediocre husband."

This stunned him. And he realized she was right. He *was* just a mediocre husband.

Garrett set out to become better. He interviewed friends whom he thought had wonderful marriages: How did they do it? What were their secrets? He looked at it as a problem to be solved the way an entrepreneur would solve a problem, and he moved from being a mediocre husband to being a terrific husband.

In a chapter about dealing with humans, I don't want to overlook the really important humans in your life: your spouse, your children, your family. I don't want you to overlook them either.

When you surround yourself with the right people, appreciate them for who they are, and take responsibility for creating the opportunity for them to succeed, you set yourself up for business success. To make that happen, you need to build a toolbox filled with strategies you can follow to get the work done.

10

FILL YOUR TOOLBOX

Split test everything.

(FROM JEFF'S NOTEBOOK)

Miyamoto Musashi was a legendary Japanese swordsman and philosopher who wrote a book on strategy for swordsmanship called *The Book of Five Rings*. He was comfortable with contradictions.

One strategy he advocated was attacking the corners. Instead of trying to cut someone's heart out, Musashi wrote, slice off a finger of his left hand, then go after his right toe, and so on—attacking the corners to weaken your opponent. At the same time, he advocated a second strategy: charge directly for the head. Exactly the opposite of the four corners strategy. And that, most certainly, was his point.

For entrepreneurs, as for swordsmen, you need a toolbox of strategies you can use to build your business. Many are contradictory—but that doesn't mean one or the other is wrong. It means you need to pick the right tool for the right circumstances. Here's another contradiction: You need to make a choice and commit to it—unless it becomes clear that it's not working. Then you need to put that strategy back in your box and pick another one. Remember, I talked earlier about building a mindset that embraces paradox (see Chapter 2), and here we are again!

In this chapter, I'll share a number of strategies that I've seen work. If they're not in your toolbox already, you should add them. I don't have advice to share on when to reach for one versus another. What's important is to think broadly when considering your options. It's easy to get locked into a particular strategy that's worked for you before. I've learned that there's danger in that, captured in the old saying "When you're a hammer, everything looks like a nail." I believe it's important to poke through your toolbox every time you undertake a new project. What if I applied this tool? That one? Sometimes you'll find something that surprises you. I'll also say this: Once you've chosen a tool, commit to it. If the results show that it's not working, put it down and reach for another one.

There's no particular order to these. Finding the right tool for the right circumstance isn't a matter of following a checklist. It's a matter of experimentation and experience.

SLOWING DOWN, GOING FAST

In the 1800s, when Brigham Young led his followers west with their possessions in handcarts to escape persecution and build their Zion, they came in time to what's known now as Emigration Canyon. There, from a cliff overlooking the

Salt Lake Valley, Young is said to have uttered the words, "This is the place."

This is the place where the Mormons set out to build their temple, a sacred expression of their faith. They found a source to quarry granite about twenty miles from the temple site, at the base of Little Cottonwood Canyon.

But Young needed to make two things happen before his followers could erect the temple. First he had to send missionaries to Denmark and other places in Europe to find and convert stone masons willing to move to Salt Lake. They did it.

Then they had to quarry that granite and have teamsters take it by oxcart all the way from Little Cottonwood Canyon to the temple site. I've lived at the base of Little Cottonwood Canyon, on Danish Road. And along this road you'll see massive rocks in people's yards just abandoned when they fell off the carts on the way to what's now downtown Salt Lake City. It was labor-intensive work, and slow—so slow you might call it impossible.

At the same time, the railroads were trying to cross the country, linking the East Coast to the West. One group worked east from California, and a second group worked west. Another task you might have thought impossible, back in the day.

The railroads asked Young to contribute laborers to finish the job—and he struck a deal. He put all his teamsters to work on the railroad. This effectively stopped work on the temple for as long as a year and a half, until the two groups of railroad workers met in Utah and drove the famous golden spike.

What he got in exchange made the deal worth it. The railroads agreed to build a spur from Little Cottonwood Canyon all the way to downtown Salt Lake City. Young could quarry stone, put it on railroad cars, and bring it straight to its destination. The Mormons took a year and a half diversion, did something completely different—and made the project go faster.

I call this the Brigham Young Railroad Temple Strategy. I've seen businesses use it, and use it well. I'll cover one in Chapter 11, "Raising Money."

THE CLIPPER SHIP

Brigham Young slowed down to go fast. Now I want to talk about the opposite: Go fast to go fast.

In 1848, gold was discovered near San Francisco. For a while, it was as easy as picking up nuggets off the ground. As people heard about it, they came from all over the world to chase their fortune, and in the beginning just about everybody succeeded.

The problem was the picks and shovels and tents they needed to do their work, and the food they needed to sustain themselves. Prices skyrocketed. At the time, the going rate for gold was $16 an ounce. But in San Francisco, a pair of boots cost $30—two ounces of gold, or about a thousand dollars today. A pound of potatoes cost $1.50, about $50 today. A month's rent for a small hotel room would have bought you a new house back East.

Smart shippers turned to the clipper ship. These were the fastest vessels of their day. Small, thin ships with huge clouds of sails that sacrificed a big hold for speed. Merchants would buy shovels, picks, tents, and other supplies back East where they were made, load them on clipper ships, and then race around Cape Horn to cash in. Even though they carried much less than traditional, slower merchant ships, clipper ships were far more profitable because they could move so much faster.

TAPPING SOMEONE ELSE'S ENERGY

When I choose my projects, I don't pick the ones I want to do. I look for projects that someone else out there wants done more than I do.

That's what led to *Doctored*, my documentary on the American Medical Association's war on the chiropractic profession. The effort began in the early sixties, when the AMA created a committee with thirteen employees who were charged with running a quiet campaign to take chiropractic down. They paid to have a book written. They got Ann Landers and Dear Abby to write negative articles about chiropractic. They changed the rules to forbid any doctor from associating with a chiropractor in any way, even on a bowling team. In time they named the group the Committee on Quackery to give it bite.

Chiropractors felt but could never find this invisible hand—until one day in 1974, the chairman of the American Chiropractic Association got a five-hundred-page package in the mail from a whistleblower within the AMA. The documents spelled out the anti-chiropractic campaign in great detail.

The chiropractors sued. The case worked its way through the courts for the next thirteen years.

But, in 1987, the AMA was found guilty of conspiring to contain and eliminate the chiropractic profession. Chiropractors celebrated—but their victory received little press and the damage was done.

I found it fascinating and wanted to make a film about it. But the key wasn't my interest. I knew there were sixty thousand chiropractors who wanted that story told more than I wanted it told. I didn't have to grow the project under my energy. It grew under the energy of someone else.

It was 2012, a time when nobody was selling DVDs. I sold two hundred thousand DVD copies of *Doctored* to chiropractors, because they would buy them ten or twenty-five at a time to give out in their practices.

That success led me to add a tagline to my company: movies that make movements.

When I've strayed from that strategy, I've regretted it. I did a series about wine because I'm a lover of great wines. It was the most beautifully shot series I've ever done, and the most fun. But it was not nearly as successful as other projects because there was no movement behind it. It had to grow under my energy instead of the energy of someone else.

THE CELEBRITY STRATEGY

In the mid-nineties, when I owned Capstone Entertainment, we focused on family-friendly children's videos. At that time, most kids' videos were simple and poorly shot. Nobody was using celebrities. We needed to differentiate ourselves.

We shot on film, not video, so the quality popped—and we used celebrities in every film that we did.

We would aim for Julia Roberts. Why not? Usually we'd end up with Florence Henderson, Dick Van Patten, Robert Culp, Shelley Long, Sherman Hemsley. We used kids from popular network children's shows too. For our first film, we produced a parents' guide that featured Dr. Laura Schlessinger, the radio personal-advice celebrity. That opened the door to her audience—that's the power of celebrity—and in our first year out of the gate we grossed $10 million.

Celebrity strategies can work because they differentiate you, because you're borrowing—or renting—someone else's credibility. When I make a movie, one of the natural questions people ask me is who's in it, or who's directing it. If my answer is Steven Spielberg, you've immediately got a picture in your mind about the level of the film, simply based on the name associated with it.

That's a key value of the celebrity strategy. I don't always use it in my film projects, but I always consider it.

The Rent-a-Brand Celebrity Strategy

In my early twenties, after selling encyclopedias door-to-door, I became a siding salesman. It was a mom-and-pop world of little siding sales companies dotting the country. There were big vendors—U.S. Steel, Alcoa—but the sales companies were all mom-and-pops. (Talk about not knowing how to play a bigger game! I was going door-to-door, too, and making a pretty good living at it.)

A company in Dallas named Amre, for American Remodeling, thought bigger. Its president made a deal with

Sears, agreeing to pay them 10 percent of its sales for the use of what was, in the day, a magical name. When I was growing up, our dishwasher was from Sears, our refrigerator was from Sears, my dad's tools were from Sears, and so was my Sunday church suit.

Under the name of Sears Home Improvement, Amre went from a single office in Dallas to offices all over the country. They became a public company listed on the New York Stock Exchange. The celebrity they used wasn't Julia Roberts, it was Sears. They weren't renting a name; they were renting a brand.

In Chapter 5, "The True Win-Win," I told the story of Scott Elder, who forgot to include his own win in that equation. Scott went on to cofound Investools, a teaching company that offered investment seminars. They used all kinds of lead-generation techniques to get would-be investors to show up at a hotel where they'd teach a class and pitch their full course on learning to be an investor for $2,500. It worked; they built a successful business and established momentum.

But where Investools really took off is when it leveraged that momentum to strike a deal with *Business Week* magazine, renting the magazine's credibility by offering what are now Business Week Seminars. The cost of getting people to that free seminar dropped; the number of people who bought the course on the spot went up. Scott followed that up by striking a similar deal with CNBC; eventually, they took the company public and Scott cashed out. Later he applied the same strategy in a deal with eBay—leaping to the front of a crowded field of competitors offering courses on selling successfully on eBay's platform by forging a deal to brand his offerings as eBay University.

STRATEGIES AND TACTICS

When MTV was born, there were very few music videos—it was basically radio on TV—and most cable operators didn't think it would work. The kids who saw it loved it, but the cable operators weren't buying. After a year of promoting, failure loomed.

Then one of MTV's executives hit on the grow-with-someone-else's-energy strategy. He set out to make a movement by mobilizing their audience: the kids. The phrase they came up with was "I want my MTV." They made the audience's voice *their* voice. It became their tagline, they used it on all their stickers, their billboards, and eventually it became the title of a song by Dire Straits.

Movement was MTV's strategy—and celebrities became the tactic. They begged and borrowed and pleaded with rock stars and other big names for permission to film them saying the phrase "I want my MTV."

It became a chorus, planted in the culture. And it literally rescued the MTV brand.

The Risk in Celebrities

Sometimes a celebrity can hurt, not help. You might call it the Oprah Effect. You work and you work and you work until Oprah endorses your product—and then your audience might dismiss it with: "Sure, it works for Oprah, but she's rich. It won't work for me."

Before people take advice from celebrities, they need to be won over on two points.

First, does this celebrity really know what he or she is talking about?

Second, and probably more important, does this celebrity really believe it, or are they just in it for the money? If people think the celebrity is involved as an endorser just to make money, it can have a detrimental effect on your sales.

The celebrity strategy works best when the product you're selling is a logical extension of the celebrity's brand. Oprah's known to have had weight control issues throughout her life, so her association with WeightWatchers makes perfect sense. The actress Gwyneth Paltrow embeds the products she sells through her website, goop, in her own credibility as a trustworthy, admirable, and well-grounded person.

INFLUENCERS

Influencers who build and then monetize large followings on social media are a new and potent type of celebrity. They, too, can advance your brand by associating with it, but only if the following they've built consists of the people you're trying to influence.

I'm not talking about getting influencers on social media to tweet about you, either. An influencer strategy can be more direct than that.

I'll give you three examples of what I mean. They all involve businesses that succeeded by serving an important set of influencers: people who attend mastermind events.

The first one is Dave Asprey's Bulletproof Coffee. Dave was a member of a lot of mastermind marketing events. They drew hundreds, if not thousands, of people. And Bulletproof Coffee always had a booth, pouring free cups of clean coffee all day long—tested for toxins, rainforest certified, mixed with grass-fed butter and MCT oil. Meanwhile, Dave and his marketing team were making friends with the people in line. Many became investors, bringing an interest in seeing the company succeed and massive email marketing lists. Now you'll find Bulletproof Coffee in Whole Foods and other outlets, and he's expanded his offerings—all from building a brand by tying into an audience of influencers.

A company called Thrive Market pursued the same strategy. It's a cross between Whole Foods and Costco. It offers healthy brands at discount prices and is now the largest online seller of non-GMO foods in the world. Thrive Market's CEO built the company for a year and a half before it actually existed. He was at all of these mastermind events pitching his idea and raised all his money from influencers. When it launched, it had all of these influencers with big email lists committed to its success.

Todd White built Dry Farm Wines by supplying free wine at hundreds of mastermind events every year. They'll ship in wine and people without asking for anything in return. His wines are paleo friendly, low in alcohol, and sugar-free. Perfect for the ketogenic diet. By pouring glass after glass of free wine at all these events, Todd cemented relationships with countless influencers, many of whom became affiliates. He's built a $50-million-a-year business without advertising—strictly by working with influencers.

I'm not advocating masterminds as the only place to apply this strategy. Begin by asking yourself who has influence over the audience you're trying to reach, and then determining where they gather. If your product could be recommended by dentists, you may find success at dental conventions.

THE DON'T-LOSE-MONEY STRATEGY

I've worked with a business advisor who's a really smart guy and has been successful for a really long time, but he's never risen to great heights. He's built a very profitable million-dollar business, but no bigger. The reason is the strategy his father gave him—one he's stuck with his whole life: You don't make money by losing money.

That's a perfectly valid strategy, but it puts a cap on your potential success. By taking fewer risks and avoiding opportunities that don't make money from the start, you increase the chances of success—and you reduce your upside too. If Jeff Bezos had applied that strategy, there would be no Amazon. For every bold success, however, there's a heap of failed start-ups.

THE LOSE-MONEY-
TO-MAKE-MONEY STRATEGY

I told you there'd be contradictions. This is the flip side of
the don't-lose-money strategy, and it's the tool I'm more
likely to reach for.

Proactiv is a successful line of skin-care products that
have been on the market for about twenty-five years now.
Year after year after year, Proactiv remains profitable. There's
always a new crop of teens who need the products, and so
Proactiv has always been able to ride the wave. Dozens and
dozens of companies have tried to knock it off.

About a dozen years ago, Proactiv started using celebrities in its advertising campaigns—big celebrities. It cost a
couple million dollars to bring one on board. The competitors thought, *Hmm, maybe that's what's making this work.* And
they began hiring celebrities too.

What they couldn't see was the rest of the iceberg
beneath the water's surface. Proactiv's average first order
was $49, and it costs the company just under $200 to
acquire it. So, Proactiv was losing about $150 on every
first sale it made.

But then they optimize the back end. They monetize
their list by renting it out, and that first order leads to more.
A sale that costs them $200 to make is eventually worth
$300. They are buying $3 for $2, and they're willing to go in
the hole by millions of dollars to make that first sale.

They're losing money to make money—and that's why
they've outlasted everyone else.

SERVING THE KING

The serve-the-king strategy is all about leverage. Instead of trying to serve the masses, you choose your most deep-pocketed customers and focus only on them.

This doesn't mean that there's not a market for Kias. It means the customers you're after are more likely to drive a Mercedes. This shapes how you promote your product, just as it may shape your product itself.

In his long working life, Gary Halbert was known as the GOAT of copywriters (more on him in Chapter 7). The greatest ever. He produced more multimillion-dollar campaigns in different niches than any of his peers. One of his mantras was this: The most important thing you can do is build a list, and as long as you're going to build a list, why not build it out of people who make a lot of money? That's the serve-the-king strategy.

THE WRIGLEY STRATEGY

Here's the flip side of the serve-the-king strategy: the Wrigley strategy. Instead of trying to make lots of money selling high-end products to small numbers of rich people, you aim to make lots of money by selling very inexpensive products to large numbers of everyday people. The power of this strategy can be seen by taking a visit to the Wrigley Mansion in Phoenix—built between 1929 and 1931 by William Wrigley Jr., who made his fortune selling chewing gum. Lots of chewing gum, one pack at a time.

I've used both of these strategies and they're both great. The key is to know which one you're pursuing, and not to do both at the same time. You wouldn't buy a luxury car from Kia. You wouldn't buy an economy sedan from Mercedes or Lamborghini either.

I've found that which approach you take often matters less than simply choosing one and committing to it. The danger lies in playing both strategies at the same time. Don't try to do both.

DAVID'S WISDOM
THE WRIGLEY GUM ICEBREAKER

When David walked into a room, the first thing he'd do is reach into the pocket of his suit jacket and pull out a dozen packs of Wrigley's Gum, some sugar-free, all different flavors, and throw them on the table. "Okay," he'd say, "before we get started, everybody has to have a pack of gum." He'd joke: "This is a psychological test that will tell me a lot about you." It was a great way to break the ice.

Turned out it had many uses too. Once, David showed up at an airport without his wallet. This was before the days of TSA and full-on security. He walked up to the woman at the gate and reached for his gum. "You know what?" he said. "You look like an angel. I sure hope so because I need an angel right now. But first you need to take a pack of gum. Which one would you like?"

David did this so often in so many circumstances that people who didn't know his name knew him as the gum man. Sometimes he'd invite me to share his courtside seats at a Utah Jazz NBA game—and we both knew he'd be late, because he was always late. He'd call and tell me to bring a pack of gum and park in the Jazz 100 parking lot. I'd pull in without a parking pass, give the attendant a stick of gum, and tell him the gum man would be along soon with the parking pass. Inside I'd approach the usher, offer a stick of gum, and tell him the gum man would be along soon with my ticket. It worked every time.

Oh, and that day at the airport? David made his flight.

THE RAZORBLADE STRATEGY

Back when Kodak dominated the market in photography, it didn't make money from selling cameras. In fact, it sold great cameras inexpensively, because it made money selling film and film processing. It's a terrific strategy, and it begins with asking a question: Can we make less on the front end with our product if it leads to serving the customer over a long period of time?

It's called the razorblade strategy because, in that world, the money is in the blades, not the razors. Same goes for printers. If you've paid nearly as much for replacement ink as you did to buy the printer in the first place, you know what I mean.

THE FIRST MOVER

If you're first in a market, creating a new industry, you've got to move fast and try to dominate as quickly as you can. There's no better example of this than Groupon, the Chicago-based group-deals start-up that became the fastest company in history to reach a billion dollars in sales.

Groupon worked by collecting groups of customers who wanted a product and connecting them with a business willing to sell it to all of them at a discount. Their first campaign grouped twenty-five people looking to buy a float tank session with a Chicago provider willing to sell a session at half price. Of that 50 percent, half went to the provider and half to Groupon. Within two years, Groupon sales reached a billion dollars.

The first mover advantage is almost impossible to defeat. To be sure, it can be done. There was a time when Yahoo had a stranglehold on internet searches—and then Google came along. But for the most part, a well-executed first mover strategy is hard for competitors to match. I don't know that there's any company in the world right now that could effectively compete with Amazon. Not even Walmart. Jeff Bezos built that position by moving first—then moving, and moving, and moving.

Back in the early 2000s, Overstock.com devoted a team of some of the smartest people I've ever met for more than a year on a secret project they code-named Biscuit. They spent big to develop what they called Overstock Auctions, a platform intended to go head-to-head with eBay. But if you go to Overstock.com now, you won't find Overstock

Auctions. That's because they ran into the headwind of eBay's first move advantage: Not only did eBay have the sellers, they had the buyers coming to their site and providing income for the sellers. They had both sides of the equation in hand; competitors like Overstock Auctions might succeed in attracting sellers, but without buyers they were running a ghost town. The value is in the network. At the time, eBay's advantage was insurmountable, and there's still no big competitor on the horizon.

THE FAST FOLLOWER

A fast follower looks at a success—like Groupon—and jumps on the business model, seeking to profit from an idea without having to take on the risk of an untested idea. This can work—I know, because I've done it.

I looked at Groupon's rise and decided to jump on its model. It was the first time I'd started a company that wasn't my own idea. We added charity into the formula, partnered with the Children's Miracle Network, and formed a business called Deals That Matter.

The key to a business like Groupon is an email list to which you can offer the deals. You can start a deals company, but if you don't have a list of people who want you to send them deals every day, then you have nothing.

Through my deal with the Children's Miracle Network, I gained access to about a hundred different charities that let us mail their list of contributors these deals on a daily basis in exchange for our 25 percent share of the deal for the first ninety days. For those three months, all the money we made went to the charity. The charities raised money without asking for money; instead, they offered deals to their supporters. It was a form of sustainable giving: Buying a pizza at, say, 50 percent off was a way to put dinner on the table for a bargain while supporting a cause that mattered. The business on the other end hoped that the customers who came in on deals would come back again. And after ninety days, the profits shifted from the charities to us.

The fast follower isn't looking to create a river. It's looking to find one and join the flow. For a time, we rode successfully in Groupon's wake. Unfortunately, the Groupon model ran its course. It turned out that a very small percentage of the audience it attracted—about 3 percent—was buying all the deals it offered. Once the heavy users filled their desk drawers with more coupons than they could possibly use, the heavy users stopped being heavy users. Groupon's stock dropped from $35 a share to less than $3 a share. Our business rode the wave down with Groupon. I sold Deals That Matter to the local NBC affiliate and left the group deals business behind.

The greatest fast follower success may be Facebook, which followed Myspace into the world of social networking. Between 2005 and 2009, Myspace was the biggest social media platform in the world—and then it cratered. In Facebook's early years, Mark Zuckerberg's guiding principle was "Don't be Myspace." Facebook rose because it played the fast follower strategy to perfection, capitalizing on what Myspace did right while learning from everything it did wrong.

The Synthesizer Corollary

It's very common to copy competitors. A step above that is synthesizing successful ideas from unrelated industries. Best practices spread quickly through an industry. The entrepreneurs who really make advances look outside of their industry for winning ideas they can apply to their business.

A terrific illustration of this concept involves writing software, which has shifted largely from what was called a waterfall methodology to the approach known as Agile development, which I've described before (see Chapter 4). From the biggest tech companies, including Groupon, Facebook, and eBay, to the latest and hoping-to-be-greatest start-ups, just about everyone in the software world has embraced the Agile methodology.

Conceptually, waterfall development treats writing software like building a building. You invest a lot of time and money creating a detailed blueprint, down to the last details, and only once you've got everything right do you begin to build. When it comes to building a building, it makes perfect sense. You don't want to get to the twentieth floor and then decide to move the elevator shaft; it's incredibly expensive.

But it turned out that developing software is nothing like building a building. Making changes as you go is not a big deal at all. At the same time, the risk in putting your head down and following a software blueprint blindly is very high. That's how you get projects delivered two years later that no longer meet the client's needs.

As we've discussed, Agile development is based on the concept of releasing early and often, beginning with the

MVP, or minimum viable product. Developers work in short sprints, or Scrums, typically one or two weeks long and no longer than four. You put every release in front of customers, and let their feedback guide you forward. Developing software becomes a matter of never-ending iteration—and it works. Agile development and MVP releases are the heart of what's called the lean start-up, now the go-to approach for tech-based entrepreneurs.

Do you know where the Agile approach has its roots? Not in software development at all.

It's a sixty-year-old concept developed by an engineer named William Deming, who brought the approach to Toyota in the 1950s and 1960s. Agile principles are at the core of what became Toyota's total quality strategy, which lifted the automaker from the realm of cheap, low-quality automobiles to the highest standards in the world. The approach became so deeply embedded at Toyota that every worker on an assembly line was empowered to stop the line if they noticed a quality issue. Even onetime projects, like retooling a factory to produce a new model, were broken into short sprints. At the end of each sprint, the project managers would assess progress and problems, then adapt before beginning the next sprint. The consistent result: on time, if not better, and under budget.

Viral marketing–based crowdfunding is another great example. A film company in Utah raised $10 million for the second season of its series *The Chosen* by preselling it to existing customers—a crowdfunding campaign conducted internally, without using a crowdfunding site. It's a brilliant case of synthesis. They bypassed the studios, bypassed external investors, bypassed the need for distributors—all by adapting a strategy developed outside the film industry. Meanwhile, other great filmmakers are still waiting patiently for an appointment with Netflix or Amazon to pitch their latest series.

THE LOCK-UP-THE-ASSETS STRATEGY

Sometimes there's no way for an entrepreneur to protect an idea from a competitor. Groupon executed its strategy beautifully, but it couldn't put any walls around it. Before long it was competing with hundreds of little companies like the one I started—and a giant, too, after Amazon backed a company called Living Social that competed in the same space.

When I'm confronted with a situation like that, the first thing I do is imagine what assets a competitor would need to take me on. Who are the partners, who are the suppliers, what are the other assets they'd need? Then I go out in pursuit of exclusive deals with these players. Everywhere a competitor turns in order to execute on my model, they'll find me already there.

This can be far more effective than a patent. And it can be as simple as blocking all the URLs a competitor would need to brand the business. Instead of just getting the URL for your brand, you might look at gathering up three hundred different URLs at low cost. Anytime a potential competitor goes looking for a domain, it's already gone—and you've got it.

THE CONTROL-THE-
CONSTRICTIONS STRATEGY

Instead of assets, you can look for the constrictions that bind your entire industry and seize control of those.

I'm in the docuseries business with a half-dozen competitors, and we're all constricted by the calendar. If we're going to release a series on August 4, we need about twelve days for a prelaunch campaign where the affiliates we rely on for email lists generate leads—people who will register to watch the series when it goes live. And the series needs twenty-one days to run.

I may produce four of these series a year; my six competitors might too. We're all working with the same affiliates—so, we need twenty-four months in a year to fit us all in. Amazingly, we're pretty friendly with one another. We do our best to come up with a schedule where we're not competing head-to-head and dividing our potential audience. But still, we need more months than we've got.

Our constriction point really isn't the calendar. It's getting on the calendar of the affiliates who do the mailing for us. These are organizations with big email lists filled with subscribers looking for advice and recommendations. If you have affiliates who can do the mailing to promote your series, you're going to win the game.

My focus now is to control that constriction by developing the very best affiliate program that's ever been seen: pays the most money, does the most follow-up, sends the most thank-you gifts, does everything we can to be the absolute leader in how we take care of those affiliates.

Identify the constrictions for your industry. Control them, and you can control the industry.

THE FOCUS STRATEGY

I have a friend in Mississippi named Joel Bomgar who read a book by a consultant named Al Ries who was a master of the focus strategy: identify a core focus and pursue nothing but that.

Joel took it to heart. He had divisions working on different projects, all of them interesting, all of them potentially profitable. He shut them down or sold them off, focusing the business like a laser on its core product. And it worked. He built his business up and then sold it for significant money.

That left him and his wife in the enviable position of deciding where to put their energies next. Joel was born and grew up in Mississippi, and he knew very well that in every economic survey, Mississippi ranked last in the nation. He decided to change that. Joel reached for the focus strategy that had served him well and looked for the big rocks he could leverage to get Mississippi out of last place.

He isolated two things.

One was to reform the state's drug laws, which locked up many people who then emerged from prison branded as criminals and could not get work.

The second was school vouchers, to improve education in the state by giving parents their choice of schools for their children and the possibility of a better education.

He ran for state legislature as a Republican, won, and has been there since. He took his old office building and divided it in half. He took charge of the team dedicated to changing Mississippi's drug policy. That's all he works on. Joel's a partner in a series I'm doing about how the war on drugs has actually increased drug use; it fits with his single-minded focus.

In the other half of the building, Joel created a different organization responsible for making the case for school vouchers. And he spends no time on it. He assembled another team with its own leader to pursue that goal, and he turned them loose to do it.

THE SHOTGUN STRATEGY

As much as I love the focus strategy, it's not for me. As I've told you before, my brain does not work that way. I'm constantly doing five to ten things at the same time. It's organized chaos. I call that the shotgun strategy.

For me, it's the only approach I can take. I used to think that was a failing on my part, until Kathy Kolbe, the originator of the Kolbe personality test, told me I'm simply wired that way. "Anybody who tells you that you're only supposed to do one thing at a time doesn't understand the way your brain works," she told me. "You're supposed to do ten things at the same time."

My business coach, Roger Hamilton, refined her insight. "Jeff," he said, "you need to be doing ten things at the same time, but you need to be doing ten things that make money, not just ten things."

If you're not going to adopt the focus strategy, you need to learn how to make that work for you. An entrepreneur who spends his time on things that don't make money is not going to succeed. If you're going to focus on multiple things, make sure you're focused on high-value things—the things that move big rocks, not little rocks.

SAYING NO

Entrepreneurs generally don't need any help saying yes. We tend to see potential and opportunity where others don't. It's baked in. We tend to be people who say, "I can do it; I'll figure it out." That's in sharp contrast to many people, who tend to see risks instead of opportunity and so have a difficult time saying yes to things. There are books written around the topic of saying yes to life—but there's very little advice out there on saying no.

I've found that entrepreneurs tend to stack up so many yeses that they find themselves in the whitewater rapids of life, struggling to keep their head above water amid all the commitments they've made and projects they've started. My biggest regrets usually stem from my yeses, not from the deals that I passed on.

A key to simplifying life is learning to say no, so much so that I actually think of it as a strategy. I recently invested time and money in a film project with a well-known person that I desperately wanted to do. But it came with an investor who shared my deep commitment—with zero experience and a high need for control. It came with another producer, too, and in the process of working with them I realized we had wildly different philosophies and work styles.

I could see the future. It involved continual nightmares as I struggled to educate an inexperienced investor and labored to work with another producer with whom I was simply out of sync.

So, early on, with a great deal of sadness, I withdrew from the deal. I said no. This is a new tool for me, a new behavior. It goes against my instincts. But if I'd persisted, all I'd have done was plant time bombs set to go off in my own future.

A FINAL WORD

I actually opened the chapter with its most essential lesson: Don't fall in love with any one strategy.

I'd say the same for your strategy. Pick the right tool for the right challenge. Don't be afraid to ask the question, "Have I chosen the right strategy?"

Be open to contradiction. Sometimes you may find that the opposite strategy will serve your business better. Make a choice, commit to it—and if it doesn't work, don't hesitate to make a different choice.

Of course, you can't execute any strategy if you can't put money behind it. That's where we're headed next.

11

RAISING MONEY

If you have a problem that money will solve and you
have money, you don't have a problem.

(FROM DAN SULLIVAN)

People always ask how I became a filmmaker. They'll
often follow with, "Did you go to film school?" and
I laugh. Not only did I not go to film school, I didn't
finish high school. The way I became a filmmaker had
nothing to do with making films. I became a filmmaker
the same way I started a software company: I learned how
to raise money.

If you can raise money, you can be anything you want
to be. Let's say you and I decide that we want to start a
new search engine to compete with Google. I know nothing about search engines, you know nothing about search
engines. But if we can raise the money, we can start a search
engine to compete with Google.

As an entrepreneur, raising money is the single point of
leverage you must master. It's the single skill that can propel

you into anything you want to be. Most people make this very hard on themselves. They ask the wrong questions. They look in the wrong places. They try to outsource the work to somebody else.

The reality is that if you're going to fund your own business, you're going to be the one who finds investors. You can't hire someone to do it for you. You have to develop this skill.

I know, because I did. And over the years I've raised a lot of money: $108 million, $33 million from individual investors, and the rest as one of a group of founders who raised $75 million, most of it from institutional investors. An article in *Forbes* magazine a few years ago called me one of the world's experts in crowdfunding, which at the time was accurate—because there weren't really any experts in crowdfunding. It was a new thing. In the Valley of the Blind, the one-eyed man is king! But I have raised several million dollars in crowdfunding, a topic I'll cover in Chapter 12. This chapter is focused on raising money from investors.

Before we get into the details, I want to put a black box label on the fundraising prescription bottle: Be careful, because this can kill you. I'll return to this point at the end of the chapter, so for now I'll just say this: raising money from others doesn't change the odds of failure, but it does raise the stakes. Once you raise money from others, you're no longer fully in charge of your own life. You need to do it. It is an essential element of success. But you should never undertake it lightly.

THE MONEY'S OUT THERE

You've got this vision, this dream, this business idea so promising that your fingertips are tingling. All you need is money to get your brainstorm off the ground. You're sitting alone in your living room and you start thinking, "Okay, who can I get to invest in this?" And you can't think of anybody. Wait—there's that rich guy across town! The one with the gate at the base of his driveway. What's his name again?

"Man," you think, "I'll never figure out how to get to him."

Here's what you may not realize.

All around you are people actively looking for ways to get a return on their money. They're staring at the ceiling in their living room, thinking: "I'm not happy with my stock portfolio. Where could I put my money that would give me a greater return with some safety?"

You're sitting in a sea of capital. It's just invisible to you.

It's only going to get deeper. Six out of seven people in the world don't have a legal title to the house where they live. Many developing countries have never developed a system of legal titles. They might have the equivalent of our courthouse, where somebody keeps a ledger record of who owns what property. A warlord can literally walk in and tell them: "Hey, take his name off that and put my name on it. That's mine now." That leaves no incentive to invest in your home and—more important—no way to borrow against it.

That's changing. I have a friend in Zambia who is working with the government's permission to use blockchain technology to issue legal titles to people who have never had a title before. This work is also underway in other African countries. They're leaping right over our way of issuing titles and landing in a better place. That's because blockchain is a far more secure way of doing titles than anything we've done before. These developing countries will be state of the art before the United States is.

That's going to do for the world what it did for the United States in its earliest years. When the country was founded, the federal government took ownership of the land in new territories. It led pioneers west by offering land for sale, funding the federal government in the process. As settlers moved across the country, speculators jumped in ahead of them. New York investors bought up Chicago before Chicago was Chicago. Real estate markets soared. Banks loaned against the value of these holdings. Speculators drove prices even higher. Then the bubble collapsed, the banks went broke, and people finally moved in. But this is how our cash economy got started: banks issuing loans and creating cash against real estate.

Over the next decade, as the entire world records titles on property, it's going to open up $100 trillion of capital that's never been accessed. That's $100 trillion in new capital entering the world market. We've just seen the US government, in response to the coronavirus, create $6 trillion of new capital. Our economy will likely absorb it.

As you're sitting there, thinking that there's no money to make payroll on Friday, you have to remind yourself to step above that and picture how to play a bigger game. You're sitting amid trillions and trillions of dollars in available capital.

THE MINDSET

The money is there. You have to deserve it. I remind myself
of that so often it might as well be a mantra: All the money
in the world is in the world.

Make Yourself the Solution

I have a filmmaker friend who is always trying to raise
money for his next project. At one point he worked for me
as a director. We would go film someone wealthy, and I
would watch as he talked to them about backing him. His
pitch came down to this: *Hey, you have lots of money! I have
a script I want to do, and you should give me some of that money.*

I've watched him do this for years, and it cracks me up.
I finally had to tell him that every instinct he had about
raising money was wrong.

You need money? So what. The market does not care.
You are standing in front of a vault with all the money you'll
ever need inside, but you will never open the door unless
you know the combination.

In Chapter 10, I talked about tapping into someone else's
energy. I don't make the films that I want to make; I make
the films other people want more than I do. The same principle holds for raising money.

My wife, Dori, is a small real estate investor who owns
several single-family homes. It's not her primary business;
she's a yoga instructor, Pilates teacher, and a personal trainer.
But it's fun for her and gives her a little security. We were
on a hike one day when she told me about a quadruplex
she'd found for $600,000, a bargain price. She was trying to

figure out how to raise the $150,000 she needed for a down payment.

And I said to her: "Why don't you raise the entire $600,000?"

She was taken aback. To her, raising $150,000 seemed like climbing an insurmountable hill. Raising $600,000? That seemed like climbing Mount Everest.

What she didn't realize is that people who have just sold commercial real estate have a tax clock running. They've got a very limited period to roll that money into another real estate project or they'll pay taxes on it. They're some of those people who are staring at the ceiling, thinking: "I wish I could find a property to roll this money into right now. And I wish I had somebody to partner with me, so I don't have to do the day-to-day operations—or I'm going to be stuck paying this tax."

Like my filmmaker friend, Dori was looking for the solution to her problem. But in reality, if she's positioned right, she's the solution to someone else's problem. And we've got friends who are accountants with vast lists of clients. They know the people who are looking for her to solve their problem.

You have to stop thinking about your project and why it's so meaningful. You can't be like my friend who says, "I've got this great movie that I really want to make. You have lots of money. Will you help me make my movie?" You have to shift your perspective. The way to find the money is to look through the eyes of investors instead of through yours.

Knowing What Investors Want

It's important to understand the basic things most investors want.

- They want predictability. Money flows to predictability.
- They want to look good to their friends, so their status goes up. They want to feel and appear smart.
- They want to feel like insiders, like they're in the know.
- They want high returns with little risk. They want to avoid the fear of missing out—but they also want to avoid the potential embarrassment of making a foolish investment.
- For men, making money is kind of like a sport. They want to win, and they love to win big.
- Women are different. They tend to value safety over return. And they want to feel good about money. They want to give, they want to contribute, they want to make a difference.

One of the ways you judge the health of a developing country is the weight of babies and toddlers. If babies are underfed, if their weight is down, the society is doing poorly. If you can raise the weight of babies, the health of the society as a whole improves. It's one of the key indicators of progress.

The people trying to address this issue have found that if they give money to men to develop answers to the challenge, then drug use and gambling and alcoholism go up—but the weight of babies doesn't. But when the money is used to fund female entrepreneurs and their solutions, then babies put on weight. It's why you see a lot of microlending programs throughout the world lending women two hundred dollars to buy a sewing machine or brickmaking machine. They've found the way to insert money into a society is through women.

If you're raising money, you need to be aware of this. By 2030, more than 60 percent of the world's wealth is going to be controlled by women. We're talking about a multitrillion-dollar transfer that's occurring between now and 2030. Pitching ideas that contribute to society will become more and more important.

DAVID'S WISDOM
ALWAYS WORK ON THE SECOND HALF

At the very beginning, when I started Talk2, it was just me alone in a room with an idea. I called David, who said, "Jeff, if your idea's good, I'll always put in the first $100,000, because the only hard money to raise is the first."

I added three friends as partners, we got the legal work done, and we set out to raise a million dollars at a dollar a share. David gave us the structure—always work on the second half—and it's brilliant. He assigned each of us $250,000 to raise. David took the first $100,000 of my two-fifty, so now I only had $150,000 left. He created scarcity where there was none before.

I called my friends and said, "Hey, we're raising a million dollars, but unfortunately I only have $150,000 left. I can't bring you in at $50,000, but I can get you in at $25,000. You don't want to miss this."

We went out, we busted our butts for a month—but we only raised $600,000. We had twenty-five people sitting on the fence, but we were out of gas.

David wasn't done. He said, "Tell everybody they have until Friday at five o'clock, and whatever's left then in Round One, David Nemelka is going to take. And on Monday we're announcing a new offer at $2 a share."

At 5:30 p.m., we had a guy run in with his check in hand, saying, "Did I miss it? Can I still get in?" We took his check. And we didn't just meet the million-dollar goal; we cleared it. This is the company we ended up raising $75 million to fund.

Always work on the second half. Structure your deal with someone else working side by side to raise the money. You've already divided what you need in half, and nobody feels like the first investor.

Momentum, Momentum, Momentum

I've talked about *On Native Soil*, my 9/11 documentary that got short-listed for an Academy Award. The budget for this film started at $300,000 and grew to $800,000. I was coming off a financial success where my investors made two and a half times their investment in a very short time. Raising money was as simple as calling them and saying this is what I'm going to do next. I coasted to the $800,000 without effort.

We ended up gathering the largest collection of footage from 9/11 that had ever been assembled. We interviewed the only survivors who were on floors above where the planes hit the buildings. Their stories were amazing, gut-wrenching, profound. I would walk out on the street with tears streaming down my face and think, "How can people just be driving by, living their life?"

I started getting my early investors together in my office over lunch to show them these interviews and keep them abreast of what we were doing and the impact it would have. They began bringing friends along, who wanted to know if they could invest in the project. I'd say no, we don't need any more money. Once I found a check on my desk chair with a note saying, "Jeff, I really want to be a part of this, would you please accept my money?"

Then we had the opportunity to get Kevin Costner and Hilary Swank to narrate it, and we had the opportunity to buy or license more footage. We needed more money. I let the budget swell to $1.7 million, and we raised that money from people who just wanted to be a part of it because of the project's momentum.

Quite a contrast to the times when you're sitting with your head in your hands, trying to figure out how to make payroll on Friday. That's the difference momentum makes. You have to figure out how to create it.

THE MECHANICS

There's nothing exciting about the mechanics of raising money. It's mundane stuff. But it's important to know what the levers are and how to pull them.

Stupid Money

You don't fund an idea, you fund a business. If all you have is an idea on a piece of paper, you probably don't deserve funding. The first round of money needs to come from you, your credit cards, your mom.

That's right, your mom.

I have a friend with a very successful medical business in Orange County. I went over one day, met at his beautiful building, got in his brand-new Rolls-Royce, and went to lunch. We came back, parked next to his Audi RS7, and went inside—and there sat his mother.

She was around because his business and his building and his luxury cars all started with a second mortgage on his mother's house. This is the sad fact: most businesses today start with the blood, sweat, and tears of the owner.

If you just have an idea, you need to fund it. You need to apply for more credit cards. The first money to start your business comes from friends and family. I truly believe that if it weren't for American Express, Visa, and MasterCard, the entrepreneurial economy would disappear.

Institutional investors have a name for this money.

Stupid money.

I don't think they're being derogatory. It means the money's coming from investors who don't know how to vet a deal properly, what returns they should ask for. It's not always given because the investors love the idea; it's because they love the entrepreneur. And sometimes stupid money can win big.

If you're going for professional investors, they have to see some of the risks taken out of the deal. As David Nemelka would say, for some people, the stock is cheaper at $5 a share than it is at $1 a share. At $1, the potential for failure is too great. Which means the first dollar needs to come from you.

Valuation

Experience has taught me that you have to know what your idea is worth. The money is the only thing that's really at risk in your business, and you have to put a proper value on it. There was a time in the dot-com bubble when a business plan and a solid management team were worth an initial evaluation of $8 million to $10 million. Just by themselves. But that bubble popped.

You have to be realistic about your valuation, because that's how you calculate what the investor gets. If you're going to raise a million dollars and you're willing to give away 50 percent of your company to do it, you're saying its valuation is $2 million. Entrepreneurs can be ridiculously out of touch with what's fair for an investor. They'll say, "We've got this great idea. We're going to raise a million dollars and we're going to give away 5 percent of the company to get it." There's no way that a company with only an idea to offer is worth a $20 million valuation.

Your Lawyer

There's a legal side to raising money, and it's both a necessity and a pitfall.

Getting your paperwork and your offer structured right takes legal help. Do not go to your regular business attorney, or you'll spend a fortune while he educates himself on securities laws. These laws change all the time, and there's tremendous risk involved.

When you're taking money from the public, you're generally dealing with accredited investors only. That means you're dealing with people who are wealthy. This allows you to use the security regulations that make offerings to accredited investors exempt from registration. Offerings to the public must be registered offerings, and this involves hundreds of thousands of dollars in expense. You're generally not going to take your company public while it's little. When it's just starting, you need to be exempt from registration.

The Obama administration produced new guidelines that let you expose private offerings to the public. But there are still hurdles to clear.

Get legal advice. Hire a securities attorney.

Disclosure

When you list the risk factors—all the ways this could go bad—in your disclosure document, don't hold back. Think of every single one you can. The economy could tank, competitors could get you, key members of your management team could die.

You need to put all this in your disclosure document, because it's not for the investor. It's for you. This is to protect you. If things go bad, at least you disclosed it up front.

The Pitfall?

Getting bogged down in paperwork. Don't let it happen. An attorney can spend six months and charge $50,000 or more for the private placement memorandum you'll use to raise your money. None of that moves you one bit closer to raising money. You can spend months and months writing a business plan, months and months creating projections and financials. It's just busy work, and it takes you away from the hard work of raising money.

A Simple Pitch

Investors always want a big private placement memorandum. The bigger it is, the more serious it looks. But the more details that you put into it, the more you'll hear the same phrase: "Wow, this looks really good. Let me give this to my accountant and our lawyer to read."

I started a company in 2000 called Thin Millionaire. I raised $3 million with a twelve-page glossy handout with photos, well-written copy, and only a graphic designer on the payroll. I never did create a formal business plan or a private placement memorandum.

There's a saying that the way money is raised is on the back of a napkin: two people sitting in a coffee shop, the entrepreneur sketching out the business on a napkin, the investor hanging on every word. We photoshopped a napkin, and on every other page we presented the major aspects of the business on a napkin. We called it the Napkin Summary.

I sent a hundred copies of the Napkin Summary out and went to work on my business plan. Investors began to call, saying, "Hey, I'm in. I like this. That was the best business plan I've ever read."

It wasn't my business plan. It was my brochure for my business plan. And I raised $3 million.

Nondisclosure Agreements

Sometimes people approach me with an idea and ask that I sign a nondisclosure agreement before they share it. When someone wants me to sign an NDA, I ask them to please not tell me the idea. You'll find this is common among seasoned investors. An NDA is a warning sign.

Offer an investor an NDA, and you're saying it's the only protection you've got. It's saying anybody can steal this idea and make money from it. You're going to have a hard time raising money until you at least get it started. Have a proof of concept, get something in the marketplace that brings feedback from customers—then you're starting to deserve the money.

Learning from the Experts

If you can build your company to the point where you are talking to private equity funds or venture capital firms, go in with open ears. I have never had a meeting with these people where I didn't learn something.

Most of these investors were entrepreneurs themselves who built a big company and sold it. When VCs invest in

a company, they're attached to that company, not just as an
investor but as an advisor. These are some of the smartest
people I've ever dealt with. Just taking a meeting with them
will improve your vision and your business plan. Be open
and willing to listen to their criticism. It's usually very smart,
and even if they have no interest in investing in your business, you'll learn from them.

Adding Value with Structure

There are ways to structure your offering to increase the
safety and potential upside for your investors. You're not
increasing the value of your idea, but you are increasing the
attractiveness of investing.

When you start out with a little business and you need
a million bucks, your first move will be to sell a percentage
of your company. When you're doing that, you're generally talking about common stock. But you have other
options. You can create preferred stock, you can create
debt, you can create convertible debt, and all of these can
have bells and whistles; you can create warrants, you can
create options.

Common stock is defined by the state where your company is domiciled. But preferred stock is defined by you.
Institutional investors, VCs, private investors, and equity
firms generally buy only preferred stock in a company,
because they want to create the rules of their investment.
Venture capitalists may say, "Okay, we'll invest $10 million
in your business, but we're investing in a preferred stock,
and in the event that the company is sold, we get a 5-to-1

or 10-to-1 return before the common shareholders get a penny."

That works fine if your company sells for $100 million. But if you raise a million bucks and sell your company for $10 million, and your preferred shareholders are due $10 million, your common shareholders will get nothing.

I want to take care of my early investors, so I always give them the right to convert into the next round if it's an institutional round. That way they can convert their common stock into preferred stock that's designed by somebody who is going to put a much sharper structure in place. The VCs don't like it, but they'll tolerate it. You can start with a preferred offering up front instead of selling common stock and write that rule just as the VCs would.

You can choose to raise money in the form of debt, with interest-only payments. Investors get a return on their money starting in a year, and at the end of two years, they either get their money back or convert to stock at a specific price. This gives investors the appearance of more safety. Obviously, if the company goes broke, it can't pay its debt. But debt takes preference over equity if a company goes broke. So, if the company is liquidated, whatever is left gets divided among the debtholders before common shareholders get anything.

You can find terrific ideas by searching online for offerings that have been sold out. A lot of these are online for angel pools. You'll find some brilliant structures and can focus on the ones that raised a lot of money. Sometimes it's the structure that attracts investors, not the idea itself.

Knowing When to Pay Yourself

If you're doing a small launch and just have to get something built by raising money from your friends and family before it generates revenue, you wouldn't normally put a salary for yourself in there. If you do, it's a warning flag for the professional investors to come.

But if you're doing a project that's going to raise a substantial amount of money and take a year or two to execute, you must put in a salary for yourself. Don't go broke to fund your business. Just acknowledge the fact that you have to have money to live on. Put it in there as a salary and don't apologize for it.

UNDERSTANDING WHAT'S AT STAKE

Okay, back to the black box warning label on the fundraising prescription bottle.

The risk in raising money is profound. I'm not talking about just the risk for your investors. I'm talking about the risk for you.

I came up with a film idea about a decade ago and put $70,000 into it. This was a time when I had a lot of investors who wanted to put money in my projects, but for this project, I did it on my own. With $70,000 into the project, we shot just enough footage for me to realize it was a bad idea. I ended up canceling the project. It was a total loss—and all I felt was relief.

If I'd gotten my sister to put money in it, if I'd gotten my friends to put money in it, I would have either had to tell them I lost their money, or I would have proceeded with a bad project because I had other people's money in mind.

Every time you raise money, you risk your reputation, you risk your friendships, you risk your spirit. The weight of it is so heavy.

Earlier in this chapter I told the first half of the story about raising money for *On Native Soil*. Because I could, I let the budget bloat from $800,000 to $1.7 million. This brings to mind the haunting words of David Nemelka: "It's not just can you, but should you?"

We invited every studio in Hollywood to a screening of *On Native Soil* at the Creative Artists Agency in Los Angeles, where our sales agent worked. It was wonderful. The next day the phone calls started coming in, one after the other: "I can't believe how the film moved me. We talked about it for hours afterward. We're not going to buy it."

The consensus was that it was a great film, but that no one was going to pay to see it in the theater. It was too raw, too soon.

I sold it to Lionsgate for much less than I was expecting. I sold the TV rights to truTV and later to NBC.

I thought for sure we would sell the film for $2 million to $5 million. We didn't. I ended up losing money for my investors. Not only did I lose money from my previous investors, I lost money from investors who had never invested before in their lives. I'd taken too much money from the wrong people.

I got all my investors on the phone to tell them the results of the Lionsgate deal, and one guy got really mad. "That's all they're going to pay us? Somebody's gonna pay!"

I'm pretty sure he would consider me an enemy to this day—and that was my fault. I took more money than I should have. It was too easy.

The risks on raising money weighed so heavily on me that I made it my goal to accumulate enough resources to self-fund my projects. I did. But even so there are still times when I turn to investors. It opens doors—and it changes the emotional stakes.

As David Nemelka always told me: "You've got to be able to sleep while the wind blows. You've got to do your paperwork right. You've got to prepare for success—and you've got to prepare for failure."

That's a hard truth that I've learned to consider carefully before I set out to raise money, every time, no matter how I go about doing it, whether it's from professional investors or the public.

Crowdfunding is an entirely different proposition, and we're headed there next.

12

CROWDFUNDING

In all your ads and interviews,
you're only writing and speaking to one person.
(FROM JEFF'S NOTEBOOK)

Back before the Apple Watch debuted, there was the Pebble watch. In the end, the Apple Watch won, and Pebble was eventually absorbed into Fitbit. But in the beginning, Pebble was a pioneer in crowdfunding. When I came across an article on it in the *Wall Street Journal*, Pebble had raised $2 million through a Kickstarter campaign with a goal of $100,000. By the time they were done, they'd raised a little more than $10 million in five weeks.

I was in the middle of filming *Medical Inc.*, my documentary on chiropractic, later renamed *Doctored*. We were running short of investors, and when I read that article, I thought crowdfunding might be our solution too. It was a film for and about chiropractors; if I could tap that audience, I could do well.

When I told my producer-director how I planned to raise more money, he almost quit. He thought I'd lost my mind, that there was no way this was going to work. "Oh, my gosh," he must have thought. "The guy who's doing my financing is now going to do a crowdfunding campaign. He must really be at the end of his rope."

But in my first Kickstarter campaign, I raised $260,000—and the filming went on. I'll share more particulars of how we went about it as the chapter unfolds. And along the way, I'll lay out what I've found to be the basics of success.

THE TWO TYPES OF CROWDFUNDING

In this chapter, I'm talking about what's called donor crowdfunding or reward crowdfunding. The JOBS Act of 2012 created a second option: equity crowdfunding. This allows entrepreneurs to sell stock to the public through crowdfunding. Indiegogo, one of the largest crowdfunding platforms, was originally designed to serve that purpose, but the legislation took so long to get through Congress that the company pivoted to donor crowdfunding instead.

Everything I'm going to talk about relates to donor or reward crowdfunding. Think of it as a PBS drive that can fund your start-up.

By the way, the "JOBS" in JOBS Act stands for Jumpstart Our Business Start-ups. It did.

CREATING YOUR CROWD

I often talk to people who say: "Yeah, I tried a Kickstarter campaign. It didn't work for me," or "I tried an Indiegogo campaign, and it didn't work for me."

They were missing the first key ingredient in crowd-funding: the crowd.

"I'm scouring the pages of Kickstarter and Indiegogo looking for causes to support and thinking, 'How can I get rid of this extra money?'" said nobody ever. Crowdfunding platforms are exactly that. They are platforms that create a place where you can conduct a transaction.

The basic mechanics of it used to be illegal. If a customer used a credit card to purchase your product, and you didn't deliver it within thirty days, you could face charges for postal fraud. But donor crowdfunding allowed me to go out and say, "Let me sell you a copy of the movie now that we haven't started yet. I'll deliver it to you in a year when I've finished it and you can participate in its creation." All I'm really doing is preselling the product without running afoul of postal regulations.

But crowdfunding platforms don't come with their own crowds. I've learned that the first thing you must do to run a successful crowdfunding campaign is identify your tribe and build it.

At the time I started my Kickstarter campaign for *Medical Inc.*, I had five hundred Facebook friends. Before I started my campaign, I went looking for more. Not just any old friends; chiropractor friends. My tribe. I looked through my friends, and the friends of my friends, and started sending a friend request to everyone with a "DC" after their name. Twice Facebook paused my account for twenty-four hours for inviting too many friends that I didn't know. But in a couple weeks, I got my friend count up to two thousand— and my fifteen hundred new friends were all chiropractors.

You need to find your own formula for building your crowd. Do you do it as I did, the hard-core way? Do you do it through viral spreading? With this first campaign, I was able to encourage all our early donors to please share the campaign with all their chiropractic school classmates. After all, they were the beneficiaries of my project.

Do you find your crowd through ads on Facebook? You can do a quiz on a topic that defines the people you're seeking through a Facebook ad that should cost fifty cents a name or so to build a list. You can do it with a petition. You can do it with a contest. You can do it with an award that you give yourself to an industry.

However you go about it, you need to build your list before you start your campaign.

PICKING A STRATEGY

I think campaigns fall into three different categories. The first and the one I like best is Epic Mission. For me, the best example of that is the Arkyd Space Telescope, a telescope kids could control from their classrooms. The campaign raised more than $1.5 million. Most fascinating to me is that the company that owned the telescope was founded by ten billionaires, people like Elon Musk and Jeff Bezos and Richard Branson—people with no need to ask me to support their cause. They had a hill to get over. But they were masterful about enrolling people in their Epic Mission: "We're going to do something extraordinary together that none of us can do on our own."

The Pebble watch falls into a second category: I Want It. This has become the most successful approach on Kickstarter and Indiegogo. If you're offering a revolutionary product that people are going to want, investors will fund that product just because they want it. The Coolest Cooler falls in that category, all the new watches, all the new drones. I want it!

The last category is a little trickier: Cool Kids. Most often it's the one we use for films. "Hey, the cool kids are all getting together for a party and you're invited!" This is tapping into FOMO, the fear of missing out. The message you're sending is that people who contribute raise their social status.

YOUR SALESMAN

I've learned that the most important component of a campaign is the video. That doesn't mean you have to do a professional job. But it is your salesman. Once you drive traffic to your crowdfunding page, the video is going to make the sale.

The key to a good video is transformation. In fact, in all your marketing copy, the key is transformation. What is my life now without your product, and what is my life going to look like once I have your product? It's not about the features, it's not about the benefits, it's about who I become because I help make this product happen.

The Coolest Cooler was created by a college friend of Brendan Burchard, a well-known personal development coach and author. Brendan wanted to help, so he put up some of the rewards. One was a day of coaching with Brendan in a group of ten for $5,000. At the time Brendan normally charged $50,000 to attend one of his mastermind events. It was a deep discount.

To me, it looked like a success. They raised more than $100,000. Six figures in a crowdfunding campaign is not bad. But most of the money raised was tied to Brendan's rewards and had nothing to do with the Coolest Cooler.

He considered that a colossal failure. They went back and reshot the video. Instead of making it all about the features of the cooler, they made it about transformation: You're going to be the life of the party; you're going to have the best family picnics—look at how great life is once you have this cooler.

They rereleased the same campaign, followed the same strategy—but after retooling the video, they raised more than $13 million.

YOUR URL

Our first crowdfunding campaign was to support the chiropractic documentary. I was invited to appear on a few podcasts and radio shows and to speak at a few chiropractic conventions while the campaign was underway. It's hard to stand on a stage, asking the audience for support, and refer them to something like kickstarter-dot-com-forward-slash-medical-link-dot-three-seven-eight-four-six-nine. Who's going to remember that?

You need to set up a simple URL, and use it as a forwarding domain to your fundraising page. I was able to get the domain chiromovie.com and set it up to automatically forward to the Kickstarter campaign. When I was speaking, all I had to do was say "chiromovie.com" and people would know where to go. They'd all end up on my page.

WIIFM

When you produce your marketing video and your copy, imagine yourself listening to a radio station called WIIFM. It stands for What's In It For Me. You have to stay tuned to it all the time.

When most people think of crowdfunding, they imagine themselves as a beggar with their tin cup out, and they say silly things like, "Would you help me do this? My goal is to do this. We really want to do this." They turn it into a pleading.

This is the exact opposite. This is Marketing 101 as it applies to crowdfunding. You always have to be answering the reader's or viewer's question: "What's in it for me?" Over and over and over. Are you asking yourself: "What's in it for the investors? Am I raising their status? Am I making them look better to their friends? Am I letting them be an insider? Am I solving a problem for them? Am I giving them a badge of honor? Am I transforming their life?"

Until you answer this question, you're not going to achieve anything. I always use the phrase, "Join us in this grand mission, or join us in this epic purpose, or join us in this cause." It's not "will you help me?" It's about the collective goal of the tribe, the crowd, not my goal.

Keep It Consistent

I believe that it's important to keep your message consistent across your video and your written marketing copy. Make the same claim, tell the same story, issue the same call to action. Tell donors how you're going to use the money, and what you're going to do with money you raise above your goal. Anticipate objections. Point to a FAQ. People will have questions; answer them.

Keep It Personal

People running campaigns often feel that they need to make their email messages look like the polished emails you get from retailers. But if you consider the emails you really read, they're from friends, and they're addressing you. Use that format.

Don't put graphics in your email. Keep it personal. Don't address a group. There's no, "Hey, everybody!" Instead, it's "Hello, Mark! I wanted to give you an update." Speak to one person at a time, just like you do in conversation.

REWARDS

One of the stupid things I did in my first campaign was the T-shirt reward. It seems very logical: give $25, get a T-shirt! They don't cost much, and it's a great markup. But you'll discover, as I did, that you have to order T-shirts in bulk, and you have to order extra small, small, medium, large, extra large, and you've got to have an inventory of all of them. You're going to go back and forth with customers who didn't say what size they are. And you're going to have to ship them. It becomes a nightmare. You've taken an interaction that was digital and made it physical. Movie posters: same thing. The mailing tube costs ten times as much as printing a poster.

Simplify your life. Do everything you can do to keep your rewards digital.

Thinking Big

Fifty percent of your money always comes from incentives tied to your biggest rewards. On films, we started setting a $5,000 tier where you'd be named as an associate producer and a $10,000 tier for executive producer, along with an invite to the wrap or the release party.

You've got to have high-dollar items, so you've got to spend some time coming up with great rewards. If I got five executive producers at $50,000 and ten associate producers at $5,000, it would take a lot of small donations to match that kind of money. Just because you're poor right now, however, doesn't mean that your audience is. There are always people out there who want gold and platinum and are willing to pay for it.

Thinking Small

Finally, when it comes to reward choices, less is more. This isn't so much about the size of the rewards as it is the number of levels.

Testing supports this. A confused mind doesn't buy; a confused mind freezes. If I got too creative and added reward after reward, I made it a chore for contributors to determine which reward to take. And they'd end up doing nothing.

SOWING THE SEEDS

At the beginning of a campaign, I've learned to seed it with people who I know are going to donate. Here's the approach: Go to ten or twenty or fifty or a hundred of your friends and say: "It's critically important. I'm releasing this crowdfunding campaign on July 5, and it doesn't matter if you donate $5 or $100, choose whatever reward you like, but will you please donate if you're going to support me at all? Will you do it on this day?" And then you start working on the second day, and the third day, because the key to crowdfunding campaigns is momentum.

The Pebble watch goal was $100,000, and when the *Journal* article came out they had raised $2 million. Instead of being afraid to contribute, now you're afraid to miss out.

Momentum is not something that you let happen. It's something that you make happen.

DAVID'S WISDOM
THE BLESSINGS OF GIVING

David was a Mormon, and he was loud, and he was forceful. He talked too much. He talked too loud. He could ruffle feathers. There was a guy in his ward—that's what they called congregations—who really didn't like him. David just set him off—and I can understand that.

At one point, this man's heart was giving out. He needed a transplant. And David was the richest person in his ward. So, the bishop went to David to ask if he would cover the cost of the $100,000 heart transplant.

"I'll do it," David said. "But here's what you have to do.

"First off, stop being so lazy. It's easy to go to the richest guy in the ward and ask him to pay for it. Do your job. Go to his family. Give them the opportunity to contribute and live the blessings that come from giving. Then I want you to go to every member of the high priest group, because I want every member of the group to have the opportunity to contribute and live the blessings. Whatever the shortfall is, I'll write a check for it."

The guy who got the heart never knew that David paid for it. A year later, he called David and asked for an appointment.

"David," he said, "I need to confess to you that you irked me. I said some bad things about you behind your back. I've even said things about you that weren't true. I want to confess this to you and ask for your forgiveness."

David forgave him, of course. And the man walked away with no idea that he had just confessed wrongdoing to the man who paid for the heart that was beating in his chest.

RIDING THE WAVE

A crowdfunding campaign has a shape: U. It starts strong, and then it drops dramatically. And as you get near the end of the campaign, it picks up again. This has two implications you should consider.

First, you need to ride the wave. Don't panic. The cycle of donations is going to move up and down. Don't flog your list every day. Let it breathe. Know that this is a long U-shaped curve, so don't get scared in the middle. Keep your list informed, advise them on your progress, let them know what you're accomplishing, remind them why they did the smart thing by being part of it—and let it breathe instead of applying nonstop pressure to donate.

Second: Make the wave work for you. Crowdfunding campaigns are usually capped at sixty days, and people make a mistake when they set their campaign for the full sixty. We found thirty-day campaigns to be much more productive. They tighten the U.

On top of that, you can extend a thirty-day campaign to sixty. Do it. Go to your list and say, "Our campaign's going great, so we're extending it another thirty days!" Now, instead of having just one spike at the start and one spike at the end, you'll get a second set of spikes in the extended campaign. We've found it can almost double our results. It always comes as a surprise to the list—and the reason for extending is always because of all the momentum you've achieved.

The Echo Effect

I wrote earlier about setting up a simple URL—chiromovie .com—and linking it to my Kickstarter campaign. It can also keep your campaign alive even after it's over.

The week before our Kickstarter campaign ended, I built an identical campaign on a competing service called Rocket Hub. It had the same functionality as Kickstarter. As soon as the Kickstarter campaign ended at midnight, we linked the domain to the Rocket Hub campaign. Instead of forwarding any visitors to the Kickstarter campaign, which had expired, we brought them to Rocket Hub. In the next two weeks we took in another $70,000, just from people who were late to the campaign.

There's always more money on the table. Don't leave it there.

PUBLIC RELATIONS

As soon as you launch your campaign, you'll get a lot of messages from public relations firms—ten or fifteen, even a hundred messages from PR firms that usually start something like this:

"Hey, I came across your page and really liked it. We love what you're doing!"

It's a form letter. They'll have something they want to sell you that sounds great: "We can get this out to our list of a gazillion people, and really help you promote it!"

I have never seen this work. You can keep your money in your pocket.

If you do use a PR firm—and I've done it—you should only use them after your campaign's a success. If you use a PR firm to drive traffic to your page and nobody is contributing, you're advertising a failure. People will hit the page and think, "Oh wow, I don't want to be an idiot. Nobody's donating to this."

Back to Pebble: The article in the *Wall Street Journal* propelled them from $2 million to $10 million. But if they'd had $30,000 raised when that article came out, it wouldn't have propelled them to anything.

THE OBAMA STRATEGY

The Obama campaign in 2008 was a masterpiece of Facebook advertising. It was the first time a political campaign used social media to raise money in an organized fashion—and they nailed it.

One thing they did was pitch people on donating $5. It may have cost them more than $5 to get that $5 donation. But as human beings, we seek consistency. We want to think of our past decisions as good ones, so we hold to them. This tendency has been proven in study after study.

Once they got somebody to donate $5, their goal was to get them all the way up to the maximum of $2,500. So, they started sending emails, and they pushed that first donation higher.

I've applied that strategy by adding new rewards in the middle of a campaign. Once I built up a big list of people who had donated $5, I started coming up with things that I thought could move them to $25, $50, $100, or even $500, because they were already on the list. Once they've donated, you're not done with them. Now it's time to dig in and double down.

MATCHING MONEY

I once did a campaign that interested a wealthy person who reached out to me. She ended up donating $200,000 to me directly because it was a project she wanted done. When we got to the end of the campaign, the money wasn't sufficient to finish the movie.

We started filming. Thirty days later we released another campaign. I asked my donor if I could use her $200,000 as matching funds. She was going to give it to me anyway. But I was able to tell potential contributors that every dollar they put in would be two dollars, because of a wealthy donor willing to match their contribution.

We ended up running four campaigns and raising a total of $700,000.

I heard from the founder of Indiegogo, who said, "Wow, I didn't know anybody could do four campaigns for the same film."

And I said, "Me neither!" But my thinking was if you have a pole in the water, you might catch a fish. If you don't have a pole in the water, you're never going to catch a fish.

Matched funds will always increase the amount you're able to raise. This is another thing to ask of your friends, the people you know who are certain to support you. Gather their money and use it in a matching funds campaign. Now you're using leverage.

THE VICTIM LETTER

We once ran a campaign on a topic so controversial that the press releases we sent got more scrutiny than anything I'd ever done before. The PR Newswire wouldn't release our material without every statement we made being referenced right back to the original sources—and we were paying them to handle our releases!

I wrote what I later came to call a "victim letter" to my list about how we were being attacked. Remember, I'm building a tribe. I wrote a letter to the tribe describing this unfair blockage, this attack, that was preventing us from raising the money we needed to tell our story. Our rate of donation went up six times.

People are conditioned to respond to negativity. I don't like this fact about humans, but it is a fact. The Republicans have been using this for fifty years to raise money so much more effectively than Democrats. If you get emails or paper letters from both Republicans and Democrats you can see it. Democrats were famous for talking about policy—we need better schools, better health care—to raise money. The Republicans always outraised them with victim themes: "The only thing standing between us and the complete takeover of this country by socialists is your $5." Finally, the Democrats started to latch on to this theme as well.

I hate to say it, but you have to consider the negative.

BEFORE, DURING, AND AFTER

Most people are pretty good at the "before" stage of their campaign. How do I build a list? How do I join a conversation that's already occurring in the other person's mind? How do I get people to my page? How do I close the deal?

Once people have contributed to your campaign, they have a new conversation going on in their mind: *Did I make a mistake? Will I really get the product? Am I going to look like a fool for doing this?* You need to join that conversation. It's a new conversation. These are the people you want for referrals. Ask them: Would you share this important campaign with your friends? Would you consider making this your photo on Facebook for the duration of the campaign? The world is full of friends you haven't met yet. Do all you can to mobilize your tribe.

After the campaign, make sure your rewards are delivered fast and that you leave your contributors with a smile on their collective face. If you built a list of twenty thousand people, and you were able to get a thousand to contribute, that thousand is worth a hundred times more to you over the next couple of years than the nineteen thousand who nodded, indicated interest, but didn't take action. Those thousand people are raving fans. This is your tribe. Treat them well, and they'll lift your business.

The next question to consider is how to build it from there.

1 3

PLAY A BIGGER GAME

All growth starts with the truth.

(FROM DAN SULLIVAN)

Every year, I pick a theme. One year it was monetization: I was doing too many things that took time but didn't make money. My underlying focus for that year was how to intentionally monetize the things I was doing.

In 2016 I had a miserable year. I made three movies in a row that lost money. I was telling a friend, Patrick Gentempo, that I really had to hustle and get my financial ship back in order. Patrick, who's now my partner, said that instead of focusing on money, I needed to double down on purpose. So, my theme for that year was purpose. Sure enough, it got me back on track.

My theme for 2019 grew out of a question-and-answer session with Jay Abraham. I've mentioned Jay before; he's a marketing guru, the best-on-the-fly advisor I've ever seen. Someone in the audience posed a problem: His salespeople made most of their money by going back to existing accounts and reselling them. But his goal was growth; he needed new accounts.

"How do I motivate my salespeople to stop shaking the same old trees?" he asked. "Should I lower their commission? What should I do?"

He did not see Jay's answer coming, and neither did I.

"On a new order," Jay said, "why don't you pay a 100 percent commission? Or 120 percent? To incentivize them, give them all the money on a new order."

The businessman was paying a 30 percent commission on reorders. "There's no way we could do that," he said. "We can't afford that. We need that margin to make it work."

"That customer is worth way more to you than that first order," Jay countered, "and that customer is worth way more to you than it is to that salesman. Your people sell reorders fine. Imagine what your business would look like if you had a thousand new customers that you could have reorders from.

"You're playing the game at a higher level than your salespeople are," Jay said. "Let them win the game they're playing, and you play a bigger game."

After the session, that phrase kept running through my mind.

How do I play a bigger game? Why is it that I make $1 million to $2 million movies when there are other people making $50 million and $100 million movies? They're playing the exact same game I'm playing. I'm just playing it at a lower level.

That became my theme for last year: How do I play a bigger game? I don't think that Richard Branson is a hundred times smarter than me, and we both have the same number of hours in the day. He doesn't outwork me by a hundred times. In fact, in all my exposure to him, he seems to work less than I do. He's just playing a bigger game.

INSPIRATION

I knew a fascinating author and entrepreneur named Ron Zeller who referred to everything as a game. That was his model of the world: everything was a game. He played games to win, and he especially liked games with a big payoff or high stakes. He viewed life as a game, business as a game—all his life, Ron was just playing a game.

On his way toward eighty, Ron actually ran a marathon while he was being treated for stomach cancer. He had stayed healthy throughout his seventies. But when he reached eighty, the doctors told him his cancer had recurred—and metastasized. He was given just a few months to live. Eventually, it was down to two weeks left. He checked himself into hospice and a friend of mine, Joe Polish, flew into town to record his final podcast—basically, Ron saying goodbye. A week later, Joe called Ron's wife to check in on him.

He was skydiving.

His son had come to him and said, "What are you doing, Dad? You're not the type to quit. I don't see you giving up on this." And they went skydiving.

Ron decided that it was just one man's opinion that he was going to die. He checked out of hospice. He put together a plan of nutrition and food and exercise, all based on the best thinking—and set out to win this game. He told me that it was the most exciting game he had ever played, the biggest game of all: life or death.

Six months later, I took a camera crew and interviewed Ron on how to play this exciting game of life, how to play this biggest game of all. Then we took him to Point of the Mountain and filmed him parasailing.

Ron lived to be eighty-two—two years past his two-week deadline. He accomplished a lot, including another book, all by playing the biggest game of all.

THE FIRST FRIGHTENING STEP

Halfway through 2019, we developed a relationship with Agora Financial, the financial publishing company, and together we released a docuseries called *Money Revealed*. It brought in $5 million in revenue in its first year, $3 million on the front end, through affiliates who promoted it to their email lists for a 50 percent commission, and $2 million on the back end, through follow-up sales of classes and workshops. We were very happy with the results.

I flew to Baltimore for a meeting with a couple of executives from Agora, and they made a proposal. They wanted to do another series, except with this series, instead of making money on the front end, they wanted to put all their chips on the back end. Their analysis showed that the back end would be so valuable that they were prepared to lose money on the front end. They wanted to pay out a 100 percent to 200 percent commission to affiliates and build a list five to ten times larger than we would normally do—and make our money there, on the back end.

Instead of a $5 million series, their financial model said, this could be a $30 million to $50 million project—but we'd have to lose as much as $4 million on the front end. Instead of making a few million on the launch, we would lose $2 million to $4 million on the series.

The good news? They were willing to take that loss to be our partner in the project.

On the flight home, I realized how terrifying this was. Instead of making a few million up front on release, I'd have to make that much to climb out of the hole before making even a penny. We normally paid affiliates a 50 percent commission. Once we raised that bar, it was going to be very hard to go back. We were looking at doing something that was revolutionary, destructive of our current business model. If it didn't work, it was going to be very hard to put this genie back in the bottle.

When I told Patrick about it, he had the same reaction: Isn't there a way to still make money on the front end and make more on the back? Can't we combine the current model and this new idea?

I thought about it all night as I slept. I got up the next morning and called Patrick.

"For six months," I said, "we've been saying, 'How do we play a bigger game?' I know the answer now. The way we play a bigger game is by destroying the current game we're playing successfully. Because the sad truth is you don't get to run to home plate with one foot on first base."

Patrick laughed. He was writing a book called *Your Stand Is Your Brand*. He had just turned in a chapter—and this was its theme.

He had told the story of Madison Park, which had been voted the best restaurant in the world. After they earned that accolade and their third Michelin star, the owner shut it down, completely, everything, even melted the pots. And he started over. If you go to Madison Park to eat now, when you step over the threshold, one of the steps is made of metal from the pots that were melted down.

Patrick had just written the story—but he hadn't thought to apply it in our own context. He embraced the concept; he had just forgotten to remember it.

MAKING THE LEAP

People leap up and start to play a bigger game in one of two ways.

The first is unintentional. Think of an egg right before it hatches. Inside that egg is a chick, and the egg is the only universe it's ever known. But now the food is running out. It's cramped, it's hot, it's too small. The air is becoming noxious. It must feel like death right before that chick chooses to peck its way out of the egg and emerge into our world. I've seen some entrepreneurs get dragged into a bigger game.

The second way is what Patrick and I did: decide that it's time to play a bigger game. That doesn't mean we get to play it. It means that we're now going to keep our eye out for the bigger game. We're asking, What is this going to look like? Who do I have to be to play a bigger game?

In a sense, you don't really have a choice; it's a matter of when you act. In my view, we're all playing a game of musical chairs. Chairs are disappearing, and people are being left without seats. You're either going to play a bigger game, or eventually you're going to find yourself on the sideline. It's the nature of business life.

The most common way to play a bigger game is sequential: you take the next logical step in your business. To play a bigger game, a successful restaurant might open a second location, and then a third. The owner might decide to franchise the idea and expand it that way. All logical, all next step.

But my favorite way to play a bigger game is exponential. I'm influenced by the business coach Dan Sullivan, who found in working with entrepreneurs that it was easier for him to grow their business by having them try to 10X it—multiply it by ten—than to have them try to 2X it—double it. If you're solving for the problem of doubling your business, you look at ways to optimize it. But there's no way you can optimize your way to a tenfold increase in your business. So, if you're solving for that problem, you have to allow for thoughts that are completely different.

SAYING NO

About the same time we did *Money Revealed*, I was talking to another potential partner about doing another financial docuseries. As we were talking, he said, "We can't afford to do promotions that don't have the reasonable expectation of doing at least $10 million. And we can only do five a year. To hit our goal of $50 million a year, we can only do things that produce at least $10 million or have a reasonable expectation to do it."

I hung up the phone and thought that through. Why does he have a $10 million threshold when I'm willing to work on projects that have a reasonable expectation of making $1 million or $2 million? When he literally can't afford to work on projects that won't do at least $10 million?

Why does he get to set that hurdle, when I choose to set a smaller one?

It really is a decision. We can all decide the size of the project.

One of the ways you play a bigger game is by saying no to anything that is a smaller game. In fact, the easiest way to play a bigger game is to start saying no to all the things that stop you from playing it.

THE MENTAL BLOCKS

You can't play a bigger game without confronting your mental blocks. They're built into your operating system. They may come from childhood trauma. They may come from your mom's voice saying, "Don't get your expectations up!" They may come from a spouse saying, "What gives you the right to do this?" They may come from a manager saying, "That's the stupidest idea I ever heard."

We all have these mental limitations that we place on ourselves. I once worked with a therapist who was helping me to control my weight. He said: "You love food so much. Why don't you weigh six hundred pounds?"

I said, "No, that's absurd. Obviously, I'm not going to weigh six hundred pounds."

"All right, then," he said. "Why don't you let your weight go to three hundred pounds?"

"No, that's crazy."

He made his point. For some reason, it wasn't crazy for me to carry forty or fifty extra pounds. Despite my lack of control over food, there was a governor in my brain. I just needed to recognize it and adjust it.

We have governors in our brain around our income, the size of our business, the number of employees we have. You have to ask yourself, what are the governors? What are the limitations I've placed on myself? And what do I have to do to remove them?

DAVID'S WISDOM
THE DR. ATKINS DIET

Once, David went on the Atkins diet, and when I came to his house, he was excited with the results. First, he showed me how loose his pants were. Then he waved me into his bathroom, where he stepped on the scale and showed me how he'd lost thirty pounds.

I was genuinely impressed. I had been on the Atkins diet myself, and it hadn't worked.

"It's not that big a deal," David said. "I've been doing what the diet book said to do and other people succeed

at it. Since I'm doing what I'm supposed to, I have a right
to expect the results."

Many people fail at dieting, and fail many times; I
was among them. Without even realizing it, I'd developed the unconscious belief that a diet that worked for
others wouldn't work for me. I was failing before I even
started. David pointed me toward a different mindset,
and it's stayed with me: if I do the right things, I have a
right to expect the results.

It's a mental construct you can apply to other areas
of life, where through the buffeting of events you've lost
confidence in the belief that, if you do the right things,
the right results will happen. David wasn't actually saying success is guaranteed, and neither am I—but if you
don't expect success, you'll rarely achieve it.

BUILDING SKILLS

Warren Buffett is a huge fan of the Dale Carnegie course on
the art of winning friends and influencing people. It's his
first piece of advice for college students, for people who want
to succeed in business.

One thing Dale Carnegie courses are really good at is
taking people who were terrified of public speaking and
getting them over that hurdle.

His number one key was preparation. Instead of
assigning students a speaking topic, he had them choose a
topic that they knew like the back of their hand. It didn't
matter what the speech was about; it could be a speech

about a dog. He'd have them do hours of preparation. By the time students stood to make their speech, they knew there was no one better suited to speak on it than they were.

You've got to be honest with yourself. Once you identify the bigger game that you want to play, ask what skills you're missing and address them. It may be that you need better money-raising skills. If you have the ability to raise a million dollars, you have greater capacity than if you only have the ability to raise $15,000. But what if you could develop the skills to raise $10 million? What if you could develop the skills to raise $100 million?

BUILDING RELATIONSHIPS

The sad fact is that the president of Sony Entertainment is not sitting in his office right now, trying to figure out how he can do a deal with Jeff Hays. If I want to do a deal with Sony Entertainment, I need to develop that relationship.

One of the best ways to build the relationships that lead to a bigger game is through charities. If you want to meet the most successful people in your industry, or in any industry, you'll find them sitting on the boards of charities.

I have a friend, Kathy Smith, who sold a half-billion dollars of fitness products in the eighties after building a powerhouse brand as a fitness guru. She still looks twenty years younger than her actual age. Kathy's daughters went to a top private school in Los Angeles called Marlborough School. It's an all-girls school, and Kathy is an all-in kind of person. She helped on fundraisers. She sat on their board.

Kathy once told me about one board meeting in which she'd been impressed by Charlie Munger's advice. Munger is Warren Buffett's business partner. People fly across the country for a chance to sit and listen to him opine on just about any topic. And here's my friend Kathy, sitting with him on the Marlborough board for years, just by contributing her time to the school. She served on Billie Jean King's board of directors too. And when I marveled at how many people she knew, it always came back to this: she knew them because she gave her time to valuable causes.

I feel awkward about offering this as a technique, but it's true: if you'll donate your time to important causes, get really involved, sit on boards, you'll meet people you would otherwise never get a chance to know—the kinds of people who play a bigger game, and can help you to do the same.

Of course, even if you sit on all the right boards and do all the right things, that's not to say that your path to success will be straight and simple. Mine certainly wasn't. Achieving success in business, as in life, is a complex and ever-changing challenge. I've come to think of it as navigating a maze, and in the next chapter I'll share what I've learned about how to do it.

14

NAVIGATING THE MAZE

You can't steer a ship when it's in port.

(FROM JEFF'S NOTEBOOK)

've told you about my days as a siding salesman. I was twenty-one or so, already a father, living in Amarillo, Texas. My partner Red and I would leave our houses at ten in the morning and drive to a tiny little Texas farm town, grab a cup of coffee, then start knocking on doors. We'd keep knocking until we'd made three appointments for the night, when we'd come back to pitch to the husband and wife.

I didn't know what I wanted to do with my life, but I knew it wasn't this. I remember telling Red, "I want an office, and I want a desk. I want to have a conference room and I want to have employees. I want to go to Miami and New York City and London, not these tiny towns in Texas." I knew what I wanted, but I had no idea what my business would be.

I thought about this the other day when I had to get up early for a 7:00 a.m. call with a producer in London. We had just taken over a ten-thousand-square-foot recording studio in Salt Lake City with a forty-foot green screen and a big control room . . . and a conference room.

I can't draw you a straight line from Jeff, the siding salesman, to Jeff, the studio owner and movie producer who travels the world filming. But here I am. I used to think of it as traveling in circles, but that's not it either. It's navigating a maze.

When you're in a maze, you take turn after turn without knowing which ones are dead ends until you get there. Then you have to backtrack and start over again. And again. And again. That's really what my career has looked like. Not a straight line, not even a circuitous route, it's been navigating a maze.

So, how do you do that? How do you get from here to there? There's really no way to do it other than continue taking the next step in front of you, following the trails as far as you can take them—and always being willing to backtrack. I hope you're ready for some more paradoxes, because that's part of navigating the maze too.

FAILING FAST . . .

Every project you put on your schedule, every idea you bring to the market, you have to think of as a test with two goals.

One is to win. It succeeds, and you stay on that path. It's something you keep.

The other is to fail . . . fast. Failing is learning, it's gathering data about where to turn next.

Both of these are valuable. In fact, they're both wins, because they'll both move you through the maze as quickly as you can.

. . . AND WINNING SLOW

The goal of a race car driver is to cross the finish line first in the slowest time possible. This seems counterintuitive, but your objective is not crossing the finish line in the fastest time ever. That burns resources. You want to cross the finish line ahead of everyone else, win or fail, without burning resources you don't need to. You don't want to burn up your tires. You don't want to burn out your engine. But you do want to race to the finish line and find out, is this worth doing anymore?

I talked about a key to doing this earlier in the book: the minimum viable product. What's the simplest way to get my idea into the market, so the market can tell me if it's going to be successful or not? I spoke earlier of Podfitness, where we added feature after feature, adding every great idea I had, before we released it to the public. I added mountains of complexity and I did it all in a vacuum. Once we released it, we learned that the public didn't care about 90 percent of the features that I just about killed my team creating.

That's failing slow and burning resources.

DAVID'S WISDOM
THE FOUR CRITERIA

One thing David often said was, "Jeff, always run all your business deals past your wife. You'll miss some of the good ones and all of the bad ones."

David had his own criteria—four questions he'd ask before deciding whether to pursue an opportunity.

Is the deal fair?

Is it honest?

Is it ethical?

And is it needed?

If the answer to any one of the questions was no, he wouldn't pursue it. The deal had to be fair for everyone involved, and it had to be honest. Of course there are things that are fair and honest, not really ethical—and things that are fair, honest, and ethical, but not really needed.

David set a high bar, and because of it he said no to lots of opportunities. But I think most people, by the end of their career, realize that the biggest mistakes they made in business were the things that they should have said no to, but didn't.

PLANNING YOUR YEAR

We've learned to make the most of our time and our resources by bringing structure to our year. We'll start our planning for the next year in December, but the plans usually change, so we'll revisit them three or four times along the way.

We divide the year into quarters, and we make sure we plan one major promotion for each. This is based on revenue. We think of these projects as tent poles holding up the corners of a tent, one for each quarter: releasing a movie in our filmmaking business, or an extraordinary promotion in our online operations. It's not our monthly consistent revenue.

I used to make these decisions by the seat of my pants, but now I know better. We've developed an algorithm we use to help us decide on our tent poles.

MINDING YOUR M'S AND P'S

We describe that algorithm as the seven M's and the two P's. My partner, Patrick Gentempo, and I took four M's from Naomi Whittle—an entrepreneur and the former president of the Twinlab dietary supplement company—and built on them. We start with a spreadsheet with a list of criteria—our M's and our P's—down one side. Then we list the possible projects across the top. We assign a number value to each cell.

The first M is "Margin." That's the difference between the cost of the product and the price it sells for. If a product costs $3 and sells for $10, the margin is $7. The higher the margin, the better the rating we give the project.

The second M is "Momentum." What's the market trend, the virality? A project may have a great margin, but it needs to catch a wave to make anything of it. I did a film on GMOs when the GMO movement was really big and carrying a lot of momentum, but that's changed. It's not very viral, it's not trending up. The time isn't right. So, we assign a number for momentum.

The third M is "Materiality." By that we mean the average order value, the transaction value. We'll sell a docuseries at a price point between $79 and $279. We might sell half as many at the higher price point—but we'll still make more money, because the average order value is so high. That's materiality.

(Why "materiality" for a label? Naomi wanted all M's, and so did we. It's harder than it sounds, which is why we switched to P's after seven. Obviously, we're already laboring. No way were we giving up after only three. Just accept it.)

The fourth M: "Market Size." We want the average order value to be high. We want the margin to be high. But if it's not a very big market, is it worthy of making it onto our calendar? What's the potential audience for this product or idea or film?

Five: "Market Access." In practical terms for us, this usually means can I find the audience on Facebook where I can access it inexpensively. If there's a large market, large momentum, large order size, large margin, but the market isn't gathered, if it's diverse, then that's going to affect our prospects for success. Is there a Facebook audience I can advertise this to? Is there a Google AdWords audience? I made the docuseries *Christ Revealed* because I knew there were sixty-eight million people who identify themselves as active Christians who we could access inexpensively on Facebook.

The sixth M is "Multiply." This means potential for back-end sales. It costs a lot to acquire a customer. Is there a logical sequence on the back end, something you can offer that customer, to monetize that relationship? The answer on the GMOs film was no; it was very profitable to release but didn't present a lot of follow-on opportunities. But one of the reasons we made *Money Revealed* is because it built an audience interested in investing and real estate. We could sell a multitude of classes, courses, master class trainings—all high-value products. It was profitable on release too—but its Multiply potential was off the charts. It scored low on Market Access, but the back-end potential made it one of the most successful series we ever did.

The seventh M is "Meaning," and this isn't a business consideration. It's a life consideration. Does this mean something to me? We're rating our passion for taking on this project. Whenever I do a film, I'm going to spend a year of my life making it. If it's a topic I don't care about, I'm going to run out of gas. My life will suffer. We've canceled projects with great numbers on all the other M's. If it doesn't have a real meaning for us, then we won't do it.

The two P's may be unique to my business. They will either apply to your business or they won't, so you'll have to figure out how to adapt or replace them.

The first P is "Polarizing." We came up with a phrase early on: "The profits are in polarity." For us, it means choosing a side. It means taking a stand. My partner, Patrick, just released a book called *Your Stand Is Your Brand.* Many entrepreneurs try to please everyone. And if you're Pepsi or Coca-Cola, if you're a major marketer, and you control half the market, then you can't afford to polarize people. You don't want to alienate half of your customers.

But when we start a new project, we own 0 percent of the market. Instead of trying to get a percentage of the entire market, we'll find more profit in choosing a side and serving it, building a tribe of people who are on one side or the other of an equation. We actually look for polarity, for things we can believe in, and we choose a side.

Depending on the business, this may or may not apply. But if you're someone starting out, it's my general recommendation to take a stand and identify yourself, your beliefs. It's the easiest way to call out your tribe.

I suspect the second P is all ours: "Production Efficiency." There may be clusters of people I need to talk to for a film that gather around conferences or workshops. I'll show up to a conference of doctors, say, where there are a thousand doctors gathered on a topic, and I can set up in a hotel room and film twenty interviews in a week for the same cost as flying somewhere to film four interviews. We call these rifle shots, where we fly to a specific location, film one person, and fly back. So expensive. The shotgun approach works better.

Once we've gone through this list, we add a weighting factor. How important is Polarization to me on this topic, how important is Meaning to me on that one? We come up with point totals. We may be looking at twenty different topics, and we need to choose four, one for each quarter. These are our revenue tent poles for the year.

RAISING THE BAR

Let's say when you're starting out you set a bar of $10,000 for each of your tent poles: we're looking for tent pole promotions that will generate $40,000 over the next year.

The next year, lift the bar: we want to do a promotion each quarter that brings in $100,000. Don't stop there, either.

I remember when I was happy to do a promotion that did $100,000 in sales. Now we need to do at least $1 million in sales with each tent pole. We would prefer $2 million or $3 million. The idea is eventually to be at the point where we're doing one $10 million promotion each quarter.

THE BIG ROCKS

Once you've got your tent pole promotions in place, you fill in the rest of your calendar by grabbing that full list of initiatives you want to accomplish in the next year and dividing it by quarters.

What generally happens—I'd actually go so far as to say, what always happens—is that you get excited about all your smaller projects, all the things you want to accomplish, and you start packing most of them into the first quarter. The result is a calendar heavily weighted to right now: "We need this done, we need this done now, we need this done now."

You need to load balance the calendar. The first thing I ask is, which one of these things is a big rock? Which of these things, if we do it now, will make everything else on the list easier? There are always one or two big rocks. If we

246 THE ENTREPRENEURIAL BRAIN

get them done, it makes everything else either unnecessary or much easier to accomplish.

I try to only keep big rocks in the first quarter. And then everything that you can push into the last quarter is a win. It's just like accomplishing it, really. Everything that I can move to a later quarter is one thing off of my list for now, which increases my chance of success. Everything you can delay is a win.

WHO?

Now you go back through this list one more time. You don't ask the how question; you ask the who question.

I've mentioned a business coach named Dan Sullivan who only does three things a day. Period. That's it. As soon as he's done those three tasks, he's done for the day. The key is that these are all important tasks. He is only allowed to do important things. Everything else is assigned to someone else.

So, now you go back through your tent poles and your other initiatives and assign someone to each of them. They own that project. It's not a task they're doing for you. They are the person who is creating, controlling, and responsible for the outcome of that task. Your role is to meet with them once a week and check their progress on the goals they set for it. If they need help removing any obstacles, you need to get them out of their way. But the project is theirs.

This is how you multiply by dividing, in the same way a cell multiplies by dividing. I look at our list of initiatives, and the first thing I ask is, "Who do I have? Who's working with me? Who can I recruit to own this task?" If I don't find a satisfactory answer, then I ask, "Who's a potential partner?" With a partner, I'll only make half as much—but I'll be able to do ten times as many projects if I collaborate and partner with others. I'll multiply my income by dividing my profits.

I did this the first time with Roger Hamilton. He uses a color chart. If you're in the yellow zone, you're the entrepreneur who is basically doing everything. The only way to get bigger is to go green. To get there, the yellow needs to start recruiting other people at their level, other yellows, and let them take control of the task. Then you're directing an orchestra instead of playing all the instruments.

It's so important—and it's so hard for an entrepreneur to do. It's easy to trick yourself. I laid out my year to Roger and said, "Here's my green year!"

"No," he said, "that's just a yellow octopus. You're still doing everything. You're just doing it through other people. You really do have to relinquish control and let people have ownership of the project."

And he was right.

I used to decide what films to do based on gut instinct. I had such faith in my ability to judge which way the wind was blowing. I was running through the seven M's and the two P's, but in my own mind only. The criteria weren't forced on me; I chose them for my own benefit. But my process was haphazard. I didn't systemize it.

I like doing many things at once, and the project I'm most excited about is always the one I'm thinking about right now. That's not a good criterion, because enthusiasm ebbs and flows. I can be the little boy who got on his horse and rode off in all directions.

Putting it on paper forced me to be consistent and thorough. We have only two finite resources, money and time. Now our year is structured around protecting those resources.

ADJUST!

"No battle plan survives first contact with the enemy." That pearl of military wisdom was uttered by a Prussian military leader named Helmuth von Moltke in the nineteenth century. It applies to business too.

We revisit our twelve-month plan three or four times during the year, and we don't beat ourselves up about it. As a matter of fact, we feel good about it. I like to say that the kind of management team I want is filled with people who can hit the curveball—because there's always going to be a curveball. The key is how you adjust to it.

CONCLUSION

Is the entrepreneurial brain a blessing
or a curse? The answer is yes.

Throughout this book, I've shared the wisdom of my great mentor in life and in business, David Nemelka, and I wish in parting that I could end with one more uplifting example of this wonderful man's many gifts and how he made great use of them. But toward the end of his life, David became increasingly manic. The driving force within that made him do great things, even impossible things, was getting out of control.

His family insisted that he see a psychiatrist and get on medication. David resisted, but eventually complied. The doctors tried several antidepressant and antipsychotic drugs. Two days before he died, David told a good friend that he didn't recognize himself anymore, that he couldn't think, that these drugs had literally demolished him. We now know that the suicide risk in taking these drugs is real, and that it's greatest when you get on them, and when you get off—the on-ramp and the off-ramp.

David was seventy-one when he took his own life in 2011.

"Our father was a friend to everyone," his family wrote in his obituary. "He naturally uplifted and brought joy into people's lives, whether it was passing out happiness gum or paying for a stranger's groceries." The obituary doesn't talk about his business successes, but about his effect on the lives of others, from his devotion to his life's great love, Ingrid, to his commitment to the cause of organ donation, to his "legendary Kids' Day adventures." He and Ingrid, their children wrote, "were true to their life's motto of 'Family First and Nothing Second.'"

Was David's entrepreneurial brain a blessing or a curse? Yes.

So is mine. So was Tony Hsieh's. And so, perhaps, is yours.

If you have an entrepreneurial brain, you are capable of great things. You are the kind of person who can make fortunes—and make the world better for everyone in doing so. But you are also the kind of person who can lose fortunes and family and your health.

I've written this book because learning to understand and manage your entrepreneurial brain is actually a matter of life or death.

That's death, from a literal standpoint, in David's case, to the emotional death that a lot of kids go through because they don't fit an educational mold that was designed to create good factory workers. They're taught that they're broken, that to do well in school they need to be drugged, that they need to be different than they are.

The flip side of this is that the people who send those messages have a point. Without a moral framework and mentors through life, those of us with entrepreneurial brains can do a lot of damage. Our prisons are filled with people who believe that the rules don't apply to them.

In Part One of this book, I shared insights grounded in my own experience of surviving as an entrepreneur: learning to live with the inevitability of failure, the reality of paradox, and the notion of practical delusion. I talked about the true meaning and essential value of real win-wins, and what, in the end, real wealth is all about: skills and relationships.

In Part Two, we shifted to practical lessons in marketing and sales, working with people, tools you can use to drive your business forward, raising investor money, and crowdfunding, navigating the maze that is your journey, and learning how to play a bigger game.

Together I hope these two halves come together in a whole that helps you better manage the great strengths and darkness of your entrepreneurial brain while giving you the guidance you need to build the kind of business that can change the world. You've got all that in you, the light and the dark, the potential to make the kind of difference that few can.

About once a year, I would get a letter in the mail from David with a poem called "The Bridge Builder" by Will Allen Dromgoole. You can look it up online. It relates the story of an old man who comes "to a chasm vast and deep and wide" through which flows "a sullen tide." A treacherous river. Experienced and wise, he crosses in the twilight— and once on the other side, turns to build a bridge back to the other side.

Someone says to him: "Why do that? You're across."

"Surely," he says, "there's a younger man who will follow me, and it's my job to leave a bridge for him."

May this book build such a bridge for you. Feel free to reach out to me. But don't stop with me. Seek out other entrepreneurs. Find a mentor. We're the engine driving the whole world's economy, and we have work to do. But we need to do it without taking ourselves down and those we love along with us.

INDEX

ABOUT THE AUTHOR

Jeff Hays, an award-winning filmmaker, author, and television producer since the early nineties, gained national attention with *Fahrenhype 9/11* (2004), a response to Michael Moore's *Fahrenheit 9/11*. He followed that with *On Native Soil* (2006). Narrated by Kevin Costner and Hilary Swank, the documentary focused on the perspective of surviving family members of 9/11 victims and their efforts to create the 9/11 Commission. The film was acquired by LionsGate and NBC and was short-listed for an Academy Award.

Hays produced a yearlong television series for Lifetime Television and then returned to documentary film with *Doctored* (2012) and *Bought* (2014).

In 2017, Jeff partnered with Dr. Patrick Gentempo to create Revealed Films. Together, they have released many multipart series covering subjects including health and nutrition, medical issues, wealth-building, and religious and political topics (*Money Revealed*, *Vaccines Revealed*, *Crypto Revealed*, *End Game*, *GMOs Revealed*, etc.).

Revealed Films launches five to six series each year, adding to the rich stream of information they've produced in the past. Revealed recently released a series on the use of psychedelics in therapy, *Psychedelics Revealed*, and has completed a new series on addiction. (Revealed Films was acquired by Genius Group, an NYSE listed company, in 2022. Hays and

Gentempo will continue to run the company for the next couple of years.)

In addition to the Revealed projects, Jeff Hays Films (JHF) was the executive producer for *The Fix*, a documentary series based on Johann Hari's *New York Times* bestseller, *Chasing the Scream*, which was made into both an Academy Award–nominated film and an eight-part television series presented by Samuel L. Jackson. JHF has acquired the rights to three other books to produce via film: the *New York Times* bestseller *Lost Connections* by Johann Hari, *The Bad One* by Erin Tyler, and *The Real Anthony Fauci* by Bobby Kennedy Jr.

Additionally, JHF produced a series with Adam Carolla on resilience, another on happiness with Ben Greenfield, and *The Millionaire Within Her* with Kristi Frank.

In 2021, JHF produced Amy Redford's narrative film *What Goes Around*, which had its world premiere at the Toronto International Film Festival in September 2022 and was sold to IFC.

In September 2022, Hays completed his newest documentary, *The United States vs. Andre Norman*, set to be released in 2023. This film covers the poverty-to-prison pipeline for people of color in the United States through the amazing story of Andre Norman.

The Covid lockdowns of 2020 provided ample time to finish two books, *The Entrepreneurial Brain* and a book on spirituality called *Love and Drugs: Tripping past Trauma into Joy,* which will be released in 2024.

Jeff resides in the mountains of Utah and works out of the JHF soundstage and studio in Midvale, Utah. Together with his beloved wife, Dori, he has eleven children and many grandchildren.